CUPCAKES

Ingrid Hancock Bjerknes

CUPCAKES

The Complete Guide to Making Beautiful and Delicious Cupcakes

Photographs by MARTE GARMANN

Translation by STINE SKARPNES OSTTVEIT

Skyhorse Publishing

Skyhorse Publishing books may be purchased in bulk at special discounts for sales promotion, corporate gifts, fund-raising, or educational purposes. Special editions can also be created to specifications. For details, contact the Special Sales Department, Skyhorse Publishing, 307 West 36th Street, 11th Floor, New York, NY 10018 or info@skyhorsepublishing.com.

Skyhorse® and Skyhorse Publishing® are registered trademarks of Skyhorse Publishing, Inc.®, a Delaware corporation.

Visit our website at www.skyhorsepublishing.com.

10 9 8 7 6 5 4 3 2 1

Library of Congress Cataloging-in-Publication Data Bjerknes, Ingrid Hancock.
[Cupcakes. English]
Cupcakes : the complete guide to making beautiful and delicious cupcakes / Ingrid Hancock Bjerknes ; photographs by Marte Garmann ; translation by Stine Skarpnes Osttveit.
p. cm.
ISBN 978-1-61608-829-3 (hardcover : alk. paper)
1. Cupcakes. I. Title.
TX771.B5413 2012
641.8'653--dc23
2012014540

Printed in China

CONTENTS

WELCOME!

I have always been fascinated by the process of making small pieces of art with simple ingredients like flour, sugar, and butter. During an exchange program at the University of California Berkeley a couple of years back, I first fell in love with the fantastic cupcakes that had become a phenomenon in the United States. Cupcakes are mini-cakes in a nice wrapping. I immediately decided to be a part of the establishment of cupcakes in Norway and started Hancock Cupcakes, which custom makes and delivers these delicacies to a growing number of cupcake lovers. I am no pastry chef, but I grew up in a family that loves to bake and where baking is tied to enjoyment, happiness, and creativity. And when it come to cupcakes, the decorations—as much as the flavor—are the main attraction, and there is no limitation to what you can create. Here you may tap into your personal creativity and add your own twists, and you have every opportunity to experiment with colors, patterns, and tastes.

The recipes and the décor you will find in this book are both delicious and beautiful—make them like you see them on the pictures or use the pictures as inspiration for your own unique cupcake creations with your personal touch. Soon friends and family will ask for your signature cupcakes for the next party!

In addition to all the recipes with step-by-step descriptions of how to decorate, I also present an array of helpful supplies and techniques that are practical to have a handle on, including preferred distributors and their contact information. Good tools are important to obtain successful results and pretty cupcakes. It's all about good decoration equipment, like decorating bags and tips, cookie cutters, spatulas, fondant shapes, colors, muffin cups, and much more. I have included a variety of decorations that may be bought in grocery stores as well as décor that may be bough in specialty stores—cupcakes should be for everyone.

Look forward to these cupcakes. Here you will get everything you need for the results to be perfect. Binge on flavors like vanilla, passion fruit, caramel, chocolate, and mint. Cupcakes provide a positive energy and bring people together. Cupcakes spread joy and warmth. Surprise the hostess of a party with cupcakes as a gift the next time you are invited somewhere; make the coolest cookie monster cupcakes for the school picnic; or use cupcakes as place cards at your next dinner party.
Have fun!

Ingrid

A little cupcake history

Cupcakes first saw light of day during the 1800s. In the United States they were called cupcakes, while in England, Australia, and New Zealand they were called patty cakes. During the 1800s, it became popular to measure baking ingredients into cups instead of weighing them, and many suggest that this is how cupcakes received their name.

BEFORE YOU BEGIN
FOR THE BEST RESULT IN EACH RECIPE

✴ Carefully read the recipe from beginning to end.

✴ Have the tools and ingredients ready. Make sure that ingredients, like margarine, are at room temperature. Take everything out of the fridge about 1 hour before baking. If the margarine is not at room temperature you risk ending up with lumps of butter in both the batter and frosting. Use margarine or butter (Hancock Cupcakes uses margarine in their delicious cupcakes).

✴ Whisk with an electric beater. This is to make air bubbles in the batter, which allows it to rise better once it is in the oven.

✴ Always sift the dry ingredients to avoid lumps.

✴ Alternate between whisking dry and wet ingredients in the batter.

✴ Make sure that you use the correct measurements in the recipes.

✴ Fill the muffin cups two-thirds full. If you exceed this amount the cupcakes will spill over the edge. Use a decorating bag or pour the batter in the cups with a measuring cup.

✴ The cupcakes are baked in paper muffin cups in a muffin pan. A standard muffin pan has room for 12 cupcakes. If you bake the cakes in paper cups without the muffin pan, make sure that they do not touch; they should be at least ⅓ inch (1 cm) apart.

✴ Bake the cupcakes in the middle of the oven. Follow the instructed temperature given in the recipe. Remember that all ovens are different and the temperature can vary from one oven to another. Check the cupcakes after about 10 minutes the first time you bake them.

✴ Pay attention to the time. If the cupcakes bake for too long, they will not taste good. Make sure that they are done by sticking a toothpick in one of the cupcakes. If no batter sticks to the toothpick, they are ready.

✴ Let the cupcakes rest in the muffin pan for 5 minutes before you move them to a cooling rack.

✴ Cupcakes should be completely cool before you decorate them with frosting. If they are still warm the frosting will run off.

✴ The perfect size for cupcakes: regular size—¼ cup (50 g) cupcake batter; mini cupcakes—⅛ cup (15 g) cupcake batter.

✴ In the book I refer to all kinds of toppings as frosting.

✴ Prepare all of the frosting and other décor before you start decorating.

* The frosting should be whisked light and fluffy, so that it is smooth to work with.

* Use a decorating bag and the given tip number (Wilton) to arrange the frosting.

* Decorate with sprinkles and other décor.

* May be stored for up to 3 days in an airtight box.

* Decorate the same day as serving.

* Frostings that contain dairy products, such as cream cheese or milk, cannot be stored at room temperature for more than a couple of hours.

Tip
When heating ingredients in a water bath, be sure to use only mixing bowls that can withstand high temperatures.

5 MAIN INGREDIENTS IN CUPCAKES

* **FAT:** Margarine at room temperature is the best for making cupcakes. Margarine gives the cakes a full and rich taste and a light, golden color. Use margarine without salt. In order for the margarine to reach room temperature, remove it from the fridge a couple of hours before baking. Alternatively, you can use vegetable oil or butter, but it will not give the exact same texture or taste as margarine.

* **FLOUR:** Sifted, white, all-purpose flour is the best for cupcakes. You may also use gluten-free flour—see recipe in the book. Be aware that gluten-free flour makes the cupcakes more compact and dry.

* **SUGAR:** Regular white cane sugar is the best variety of sugar for cupcakes. Some choose to use burnt sugar because it is more flavorful and creates a lovely, caramel-like color. As a replacement for sugar, or as an addition, you can use honey, maple syrup, and light or dark syrup.

* **BAKING POWDER/BAKING SODA:** Baking powder is a mixture of baking soda, starch, and sour salts and is used to make the cupcakes rise and be fluffy. You can use baking soda instead of baking powder (1 tsp baking soda = 2 tsp baking powder).

* **EGGS:** Eggs at room temperature from cage-free hens are the best choice for cupcakes. Eggs should be whipped with an electric beater unless otherwise instructed in the recipe.

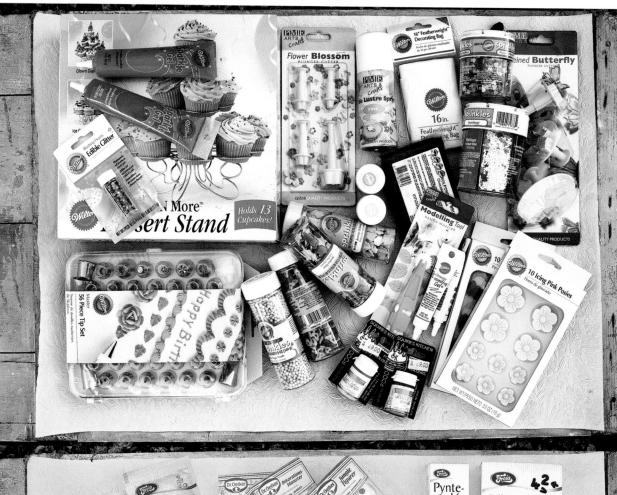

IMPORTANT DECORATING SUPPLIES

Cupcakes are known for their festive decorations, which make them small pieces of art. There is an infinite number of decorative possibilities with edible décor, figures, glitter, or sprinkles. In this book I have used decor that you can find at many online retailers. I want you to have the opportunity to make exactly what you see in the pictures. You can get the decor from the online retail outlets listed on pp. 30-31, or from a local retailer. There are heaps of lovely décor out there, but remember that cupcake décor can also be something as simple and healthy as chopped nuts or fresh berries!

- ☆ Decorating bags and tips
- ☆ Spatulas
- ☆ Paper muffin cups
- ☆ Cookie cutters/shapes
- ☆ Decorative borders
- ☆ Letters and numbers
- ☆ Templates and stencils

- ☆ Marzipan
- ☆ Fondant (soft sugar paste). Fondant is a soft sugar paste that is great for making figures and flowers, as well as covers. The fondant needs to be rolled out. Use a patterned rolling pin if you want to make a patterned fondant—the result looks great! Place the fondant between two sheets of parchment paper when you roll it out to avoid dust. Store the fondant in an airtight plastic bag; if not, it will harden.
- ☆ Food color/pasta color
- ☆ Sprinkles (various kinds; for instance, edible glitter dust. Edible glitter dust is fabulous to sprinkle on top of the frosting. To give fondant decorations or flower décor an extra sparkle you may brush them with glitter dust, either in the middle or along the edges. To make the glitter dust stick properly, first brush with water or egg whites.)

TOPPINGS

Topping (also known as frosting or buttercream) is what we use in this book to decorate the cupcakes. Its texture is soft and smooth and should not stiffen or harden. A typical frosting will consist of margarine, sifted powdered sugar, vanilla sugar, and a liquid. The liquid is often a flavor component such as lemon juice, coconut milk, or fruit juice. Margarine and powdered sugar should always be stirred white. The liquid should be added a little at a time. The frosting is then whipped light, fluffy, and smooth to work with. Remember that if you are adding food color you may need to adjust the dry ingredients, since the food coloring is a liquid. I recommend Wilton's colors, because they will not influence the texture. If you want to make flowers or borders that should harden, use royal icing.

⭐ **FROSTING/BUTTERCREAM** is the most commonly used topping on cupcakes, and it is applied with a decorating bag or with a spatula. You can use premade frosting from the stores, but it will taste the best if you make it yourself, because it's fresher. The frosting has a soft, creamy texture, is easy to apply, and the ingredients are all available in convenience stores—powdered sugar, milk, cream cheese, margarine, and the like. The frosting can be shaped to preference, since it has a firm texture that prevents it from "melting." See the recipes for specific cupcakes.

⭐ **WHIPPED CREAM** with the taste of vanilla, citrus fruits, honey, or similar is especially tasty on cupcakes with a fruity taste. Use whipping cream whipped completely stiff.

⭐ **FONDANT** is bought in squares and needs to be kneaded before you can work with it. If you want to create figures and shapes like stars, hearts, circles, and so on, roll out the fondant to a thickness of $\frac{1}{16}$ inch. You may also use fondant for 3-D figures or flowers. In that case use cookie cutters.

⭐ **MARZIPAN** basically works the same way as fondant and has the same function. Marzipan may be bought premade and works great as a decoration and for making figures.

⭐ **ROYAL ICING** is used for edgings, text, flowers, and the like on cupcakes. Royal icing dries and hardens fast. It is important that the icing has the right texture for its use:
• To make flowers, roses, or the like, use a stiff icing.
• To make edgings I recommend a medium-stiff icing.
• To write text such as "Happy Birthday," you need to use a thinner icing so that you can shape the letters in a smooth way.

ROYAL ICING
1 egg white
½ tsp lemon juice
1 ½ cups (192 g) powdered sugar

Whisk the egg whites on medium speed for 2 to 3 minutes. Add the lemon juice. Sift in the powdered sugar until you have the desired texture. You may also color the icing. I recommend the colors from Wilton. This way the icing will keep its texture no matter how much color you add.

Especially important when decorating cupcakes

☀ The texture of the frosting or icing
☀ The angle of the decorating bag
☀ The amount of frosting you squeeze out of the decorating bag

HOW TO USE THE DECORATING BAG

☆ The result depends on the texture of the frosting, but also on how you hold the decorating bag and how you use it.

☆ If you wish to make edgings, leafs, or text, hold the bag at a 45-degree angle in relation to the surface you are working with (for instance the top or the edge of the cake).

☆ If you are making stars or flowers, hold the bag perpendicular to the surface—in other words, at a 90-degree angle from the surface.

☆ Work clockwise in circular motions. If you are left-handed, work counterclockwise.

☆ Keep an even pressure while you work.

A decorating tip

The decorating bag is a classic when it comes to decorating cupcakes. All of the tips that are used in this book have product numbers from Wilton. Use the adapter that comes with the decorating bag. This way you can switch tips and make different patterns with the frosting without changing the decorating bag. The adapter consists of two parts: a base and a ring. The base should go on the inside of the decorating bag, while the ring holds the tip in place on the outside.

The swirl

★ Use a decorating bag with tip no. 1B. Hold the decorating bag straight down, pointing at the surface of the cupcake.

★ Start squeezing out frosting along the edge and work towards the middle in circles. When you reach the middle, release the pressure and pull the bag straight up.

★ Make a new swirl on the inside and partly on top of the other to make an extra-rich swirl.

★ To make a rose, start in the middle of the cake and work outwards, as shown in the picture.

Striped frosting

The base is a white frosting.
* Choose the colors you want for the stripes, and find a narrow brush.
* Find the decorating bag and the desired tip.
* Brush the colors in small stripes on the inside of the decorating bag.
* Carefully scoop the frosting into the bag. Use a spatula.

Frosting grass

* Use tip no. 233 and fill the decorating bag with green frosting.
* Hold the bag at a 90-degree angle against the surface.
* Hold the tip against the surface, and squeeze out the frosting while at the same time pulling the bag upwards.
* Stop when you think the grass is the right length. Make the grass dense.

Figures

* Use any kind of cookie cutters.
* Roll out fondant or marzipan to a thickness of about $\frac{1}{16}$ inch, and press out shapes.

Roses

⭐ Roll the fondant/marzipan out 1⁄16 inch thick. Roll a marble, and make a rain drop shape as a base for the rose.

⭐ Cut out petals with a rounded cookie cutter. Use a spoon and press it against the edge of half the petal with careful, circular movements to make it thinner.

⭐ Wrap the petals around the rain-drop-shaped base. Start with two petals against each other and continue, one at a time, until you have the desired size.

⭐ Spray with PME color spray for an extra glitter effect.

HOW TO COLOR FROSTING

I recommend Wilton's paste colors over standard food coloring. The color paste doesn't influence the texture of the frosting, and you can find them in every color of the rainbow. First, prepare the frosting.

★ Choose the color you wish to use.
★ If you want to use multiple colors, divide the frosting in multiple bowls.
★ Use a small spoon when you add the color to the frosting. Use a new spoon each time you add a new color so that the color stays clean.
★ The color of the frosting will be most vibrant 2 to 3 hours after you've added it.
★ Scoop the frosting into a decorating bag with the right tip and decorate away!

HOW TO COLOR MARZIPAN AND FONDANT

* Knead the mass until soft and smooth.
* Add the desired color, and keep kneading until the color is evenly distributed. Feel free to use powderless latex gloves.

Color tips

✻ Light colors may fade. Cupcakes with
light-colored marzipan/fondant should be stored in a dark place.
✻ If you want deep colors like red or black, you'll need to add more color than usual.
✻ The colors can stain. Use powderless latex gloves and work on a surface
that can survive some color stains. Most stains can be
removed with water and soap.

Boxes and pretty accessories

Cupcakes are all about presentation and the right packaging, in addition to the delicious taste. Cupcakes are perfect as a hostess gift or a birthday gift, and in such cases it is extra special to have them wrapped in a nice box. Luckily there are cupcake boxes sold in different sizes and design. A beautiful silk ribbon around the box is the last little touch. If you want to keep the cupcakes in a tray where they won't touch while traveling, there are muffin pans that can carry up to 20 cakes. You may also serve cupcakes on a stylish stand and in beautiful silicone cups. Wrappers are nice looking as well; with wrappers you can even make decorative edgings around the cupcakes.

WHEN THE TOOLS COUNT

Supplies, decorations, and décor that can be used to create the cupcakes in this book can be found at the following websites:

THE BAKER'S KITCHEN
Offers cupcake kits, laser-cut decorative wrappers, display stands, decorating sets, colorful rings and picks, and various edible decorations.
www.thebakerskitchen.net/

B.C. PRODUCTS
Provides cake, candy, and wedding decorations like candy oils, setter sticks, and lace doilies.
www.acbcproducts.com/

CAKE DECORATING COMPANY
Provides edible cupcake photo images, baking cups and molds, edible chocolate transfers, sprinkles, glitters, and pearls.
www.thecakedecoratingcompany.co.uk/

CK PRODUCTS
Distributes imported and domestic products for cake decorating and candy making, including candy beads, edible glitter, cake jewelry, and diamond rhinestone wraps.
www.ckproducts.com/

DAWN FOOD PRODUCTS, INC.
Offers non-dairy icings, extracts, emulsions, and colors, fillings, and fruit bit concentrates.
www.dawnfoods.com/

DR. OETKER
Provides a variety of baking aids, such as ingredients, flavoring, glazes, and sauces.
www.oetker.us/

LUCKS FOOD DECORATING COMPANY
Offers an assortment of edible decorations in shapes like butterflies, hot air balloons, animals, ribbons, flowers, and many more.
www.lucks.com/index.htm

NIAGARA DISTRIBUTORS, INC.
Offers a full line of baking products, including baking treatments, piping gels, toppings, and decorettes.
www.niagaradistributors.com/

N.Y. CAKE & BAKING DISTRIBUTOR
Offers gum paste cutters and tools, silver and gold dragees, petal dusts, silver and gold powder, chocolate molds, and many other hard-to-find items.
www.nycake.com/

PFEIL & HOLING
Offers all the supplies you'll need for baking, like novelty cake decorations, royal icing roses, cake top ornaments, and gumpaste flowers.
www.cakedeco.com

SUGARSHACK

Offers everything you need to decorate cupcakes, cakes, and cookies, as well as carriers, ribbons, wrappers, stands, and fancy toppers to give your creations a beautiful presentation.
www.sugarshack.co.uk/

WILTON INDUSTRIES

For all your cupcake decorating and baking needs, including icing bags, food coloring, fondant, paper cups, baking pans, decorations, and tips.
www.wilton.com/

THE RECIPES

CUPCAKES WITH MILK CHOCOLATE CANDIES

Milk chocolate candies are great as decorations. The various colors make it possible to make colorful cupcakes. We have chosen here to use the milk-chocolate non-stops (the Norwegian equivalent to plain M&M's). This design is great for a party, both for the little ones and the grownups. You may also use Smarties instead of chocolate candies if you wish!

{18 CUPCAKES}

You need:

THE BATTER

4 eggs
1 cup (225 g) margarine, room temperature
1 cup (190 g) sugar
3 tsp baking powder
1 tsp vanilla extract
1 ½ cups (200 g) white all-purpose flour
1 cup (200 g) milk chocolate candies, crushed

THE FROSTING

⅔ cup (150 g) margarine, room temperature
6 tbsp milk
7 oz (200 g) dark chocolate, melted and cooled
1 cup (200 g) milk chocolate candies
3 ¾ cups (450 g) powdered sugar

Preparation:

- Preheat the oven to 135°F/175°C.
- Place 18 muffin cups in a muffin pan.
- Whisk egg and sugar until fluffy. Add the flour, baking powder, margarine, and vanilla extract. Use a mixer to mix well for a couple of minutes. Add the crushed candies.
- Fill the muffin cups half full.
- Bake the cupcakes in the oven for about 20 minutes.
- Remove them from the oven and let them cool in the pan for about 5 minutes. Move them onto a cooling rack and let them cool completely.

FROSTING
- Melt the chocolate while stirring in a small saucepan on low heat.
- Cool the chocolate and stir in the margarine and milk, alternating with the powdered sugar.
- Whisk the frosting to a velvety texture.

DECORATIONS
- Add the frosting to a decorating bag. Use tip no. 1C.
- Start in the middle and immediately work your way outwards. The goal here is to create an indent in the middle.
- Fill the indent with the candies in multiple colors. If you wish you may crush them first.
- If you prefer a colored frosting, you may use white chocolate and add food coloring. Follow the process as you did above.

LIME CUPCAKES

Summer is the perfect time for cupcakes. Bring these fresh lime cupcakes to a picnic in the park or serve at your garden party.

{12 CUPCAKES}

You need:

THE BATTER
2 eggs
½ cup (125 g) margarine, room temperature
1 ¼ cups (252 g) sugar
2 cups (238 g) white all-purpose flour, sifted
salt, a small pinch
1 ¼ tsp baking powder
¾ cup (173 ml) sour milk
3 tbsp lime juice, freshly squeezed
1 tbsp lime zest, grated

THE FROSTING
½ cup (125 g) margarine
1 cup (250 g) cream cheese
1 tsp vanilla extract
2 ½ to 3 cups (250 to 300 g) powdered sugar, sifted
1 tbsp lime juice, freshly squeezed
1 tbsp lime zest

Preparation:

- Preheat the oven to 350°F/175°C.
- Place 12 muffin cups in a muffin pan.
- Whisk margarine and sugar until white.
- Add eggs, one at a time, and whisk well.
- Alternately, sift flour, baking powder, and salt, then add the milk.
- Add the lime juice and lime zest. Mix well.
- Fill the muffin cups two-thirds full.
- Bake the cakes in the middle of the oven for about 20 minutes.
- Remove the muffin pan from the oven and leave the muffins to cool in the pan for about 5 minutes. Place the cupcakes on a cooling rack to cool completely.

THE FROSTING
- Whisk together the margarine and cream cheese.
- Add powdered sugar, lime juice, lime zest, and vanilla.
- Blend well. The frosting should have a smooth texture.

DECORATING
- Scoop the frosting into a decorating bag. Use tip no. 1M.
- Start along the outer edges and work the decorating bag towards the middle of the cupcake in a circular motion. Keep even pressure by squeezing at the back of the bag.
- Anchor: Roll out the fondant, ¹⁄₁₆ inch thick. Use a sharp knife to cut the fondant into strips. Cut them in the size you want the anchor to be. Hold the spray at a slight distance, to prevent the fondant from becoming too moist. Let the fondant dry. Place the anchor as illustrated in the photo.
- Maritime stripes: Roll out the fondant. Use a circle-shaped cookie cutter and press out a circular piece. Cut small strips of white fondant; use a knife to adjust the length of the stripes. Brush the stripes with a moist brush to make them stick better to the fondant circle.
- Stars and flowers: Roll out red fondant, and use star- and flower-shaped cookie cutters.

BERRY CUPCAKES

We are proud of our beautiful country and the natural raw materials it offers. Norwegian berries are wonderfully fresh and flavorful. Berries and cupcakes are a natural match. Try this recipe with a crumble topping.

{12 CUPCAKES}

You need:

THE BATTER
1 egg
3 cups (360 g) white all-
   purpose flour
⅔ cup (150 g) brown sugar
a pinch of salt
2 tsp baking powder
½ cup (115 g) margarine,
   room temperature
1 ¼ cups (¼ quart) milk

THE BERRY FILLING
2 tbsp water
3 tbsp sugar
½ tsp lemon juice
2 ¾ cups (400 g) mixed
   berries (blueberries,
   blackberries, raspberries,
   and strawberries)

THE CRUMBLE TOPPING
4 tbsp oats
3 tbsp brown sugar
2 tbsp margarine, melted
4 tbsp white all-purpose
   flour
1 tbsp lemon juice

Preparation:

- Preheat the oven to 390°F/200°C.
- Place 12 muffin cups in a muffin pan. If possible use silicone baking cups.

THE BERRY FILLING
- Bring the berry mix to a boil and let it cool.

THE CRUMBLE TOPPING
- Melt the margarine and let it cool.
- Blend oats, sugar, flour, and lemon juice with the margarine and set aside.

THE BATTER
- Blend flour, sugar, salt, and baking powder.
- In another bowl, whisk the egg white until airy with an electric beater. Add the milk and the margarine. Continue whisking on medium speed.
- Add the dry ingredients and whisk into a smooth and soft batter.
- Fill the muffin cups about half full.
- Add a spoonful of berries to each cup.
- Cover the filling with additional batter.
- Add the crumble topping on each cupcake.
- Bake in the oven for about 20 minutes.
- Cool them in the pan for about 5 minutes.
- Serve the cupcakes warm with fresh berries and vanilla sauce/ice cream.

CUPCAKES WITH MAPLE SYRUP

The 17th of May is a celebratory occasion in Norway for both young and the old. The traditional May 17 breakfast table should overflow with salmon and scrambled eggs, strawberries, ice cream, and, of course, cupcakes with Norwegian flags. Hurray for the 17th of May!

{24 CUPCAKES}

You need:

THE BATTER
3 eggs
2 cups (350 g) sugar
1 cup (250 g) margarine, room temperature
1 tbsp baking powder
1 tsp cinnamon
1 cup (¼ liter) milk
3 cups (370 g) white all-purpose flour
¼ tsp salt
1 tsp vanilla extract
1 ¾ cups (200 g) crushed walnuts

THE FROSTING
3 yolks
1 cup (¼ liter) maple syrup
⅔ cup (150 g) margarine, room temperature
2 to 2 ½ cups (250 to 300 g) powdered sugar
2 tbsp cocoa powder

Preparation:

- Preheat the oven to 350°F/175°C.
- Place 24 muffin cups in two muffin pans.
- Whisk the margarine and sugar until white and airy.
- Add the eggs, one at a time. Whisk well between each egg.
- Add the vanilla extract.
- In another bow, sift flour, salt, cinnamon, and baking powder.
- Blend the dry mixture with the batter, alternating with milk.
- Stir in the crushed walnuts.
- Fill the muffin cups half full.
- Bake the cupcakes in the oven for about 20 minutes.
- Remove them from the oven and cool the cupcakes in the pan for about 5 minutes. Move them onto a cooling rack, and let them cool completely.

THE FROSTING
- Whisk yolks on high speed for about 4 minutes.
- Warm the maple syrup in a saucepan until it starts puttering. Turn the heat down and stir continuously for about 5 minutes on low to medium heat.
- Cool the syrup but make sure that it doesn't stiffen.
- Pour the syrup in the egg mixture while whisking.
- Add the sifted powdered sugar and cocoa powder alternately with the syrup.
- Add the margarine a little at a time, and mix well until the frosting has obtained a spreadable texture.

DECORATING
- Cover the cupcakes with a thick layer of frosting. Use a silicone spatula to obtain an even and nice looking surface.
- An alternative to pouring the syrup over the cupcakes may be: Chop the walnuts and sprinkle them on top of the cupcake, or roll the cupcake in the crushed walnuts so that they fasten along the edge.
- Carefully stick the Norwegian flags in the cream.
- Use 17th of May muffin cups if desired!

STRAWBERRY AND LIME CUPCAKES

Amaze with cupcakes instead of the traditional wedding cake. You can choose the color and design. Be inspired by this lovely combination of strawberries, lime, and meringue frosting. Congratulations on your big day!

{12 CUPCAKES}

You need:

THE BATTER

2 eggs
1 cup (200 g) sugar
1 ½ cups (198 g) white all-purpose flour
1 tbsp grated lime zest
1 stick (125 g) margarine, room temperature
1 tsp baking powder
a pinch of salt
½ cup (127 g) plain yogurt
the juice of ½ lime
½ cup (125 g) strawberry puree (pure fresh strawberries)

THE FROSTING

3 egg whites
⅓ cup (70 g) sugar
1 tbsp grated lime zest
juice of 1 lime
⅓ tsp cream of tartar
1 cup (250 g) margarine, room temperature
powdered sugar

Preparation:

- Preheat the oven to 350°F/175°C.
- Place 12 muffin cups in a muffin pan.
- Blend the flour, baking powder, and salt.
- In another bowl, whisk the margarine, sugar, and lime zest until light and airy.
- Add the eggs, one at a time. Stir well between each egg.
- Fold half of the dry mix into the batter. Add the yogurt and blend well.
- Fold in the remainder of the dry ingredients and alternate with the strawberry puree mixed with the lime juice. Whisk for about 3 minutes.
- Fill the muffin cups half full.
- Bake the cupcakes in the oven for 18 to 22 minutes.
- Remove from the oven and cool in the pan for about 5 minutes.

THE FROSTING

- Whisk sugar, egg whites, and cream of tartar well. Place the bowl in a water bath (max temperature 167°F/75°C). Do not allow the water to boil. Whisk continuously. The egg whites should not become lumpy. The blend is ready when it has obtained a foamy consistency.
- Use a mixture on high speed for 4 minutes.
- In a separate bowl, whisk half of the margarine with one-third of the meringue mixture. Mix well.
- Add the rest of the margarine for a firmer texture.
- Fold in the remainder of the meringue mixture and whisk well.
- Add the grated lime zest and lime juice. Blend well.
- Sift the powdered sugar in the bowl a little at a time. Add enough powdered sugar so that the frosting has a nice taste and is easily spreadable.

DECORATING

- Place the frosting in a decorating bag. Use tip no. 1M.
- Start on the outer edge and shape the frosting towards the middle into a peak.
- Decorate with pear spray, glitter dust, pears, flowers, and so on.

MARSHMALLOW CUPCAKES

Marshmallows make the cupcakes extra soft. The small silky-soft pillows give a full and airy frosting reminiscent of a beautiful winter wonderland. Decorate with snow crystals and edible glitter, and you'll have a wonderful winter temptation.

{12 CUPCAKES}

You need:

THE BATTER
1 egg
¾ cup (150 g) sugar
1 cup (130 g) white all-purpose flour, sifted
1 ½ tsp baking powder
¼ cup (55 g) margarine, room temperature
½ cup milk
1 tsp vanilla extract

FILLING
12 white marshmallows, large

FROSTING
⅓ cup (80 g) margarine, room temperature
2 ½ cups (250 g) powdered sugar, sifted
3 ½ tbsp milk
½ tsp vanilla extract
2 cups (100 g) mini marshmallows, white

Preparation:

- Preheat the oven to 350°F/175°C.
- Place 12 cupcake baking cups in a baking sheet.
- Whisk eggs and sugar until light and airy.
- Blend margarine, baking powder, and vanilla extract in a separate bowl.
- Alternately add flour and milk to the margarine mixture.
- Add the egg-and-sugar blend in with the batter and whisk well for about 1.5 minutes on medium speed.
- Fill the baking cups halfway.
- Bake the cupcakes in the oven for about 20 minutes.
- Remove them from the oven and let them cool in the baking sheet for about 5 minutes before you move them over to a cooling rack.
- When the cupcakes are completely cool, make a small hole in the middle of each cupcake with an olive pitter. Make sure that you don't push the pitter through the bottom of the cupcake. The hole will now be filled with marshmallow filling.

THE FILLING
- Melt the marshmallows in a water bath. Cool.
- Squeeze the marshmallow fill into the cupcakes by using a decorating bag.

FROSTING
- Whisk margarine, milk, sifted powdered sugar, and vanilla extract.
- Whisk until the mixture has a thick, buttery texture. Add the mini marshmallows and stir with a ladle.

DECORATING
- Add the frosting to the cupcakes with a spatula. The marshmallows will make the frosting uneven.
- Sprinkle snow crystals and edible glitter on top.

DAIM CUPCAKES

The Daim chocolate is very popular, and it is a blend of almond brittle and milk chocolate (similar to Skor in the United States). Children will love these Daim cupcakes for their birthday parties, and if there are any leftovers I am sure the grownups will be happy to try some too.

{12 CUPCAKES}

You need:

THE BATTER:
3 eggs
1 cup (210 g) sugar
1 tsp vanilla sugar
½ cup (100 g) margarine, room temperature
⅓ cup (100 ml) milk
1 tbsp cocoa powder
1 ½ cups (184 g) white all-purpose flour
2 tsp baking powder
1 small pinch of salt
5 to 7 oz (150 to 200 g) Daim or Skor, sliced in small pieces

THE FROSTING
½ cup (100 g) margarine
3 cups (350 g) powdered sugar
3 ½ tbsp milk
3 tbsp caramel sauce
1 tbsp cocoa powder
3.5 oz (100 g) Daim or Skor, broken into pieces

Preparation:

- Preheat the oven to 350°F/175°C.
- Place 12 muffin cups in a muffin pan.
- Whisk eggs and sugar until stiff and fluffy.
- Alternate between adding the milk and the dry ingredients.
- Fold in the chopped chocolate.
- Fill the muffin cups half full.
- Sprinkle Daim or Skor pieces on top.
- Bake the cakes in the middle of the oven for 16 to 20 minutes.
- Remove them from the oven and cool in the pan for about 5 minutes. Place the cupcakes on a cooling rack, and let them cool completely.

THE FROSTING
- Stir the margarine and half of the powdered sugar white.
- Add the milk, the remaining powdered sugar, cocoa powder, and caramel sauce. Whisk well. Turn in the Daim/Skor pieces.

DECORATING
- Place the frosting in a decorating bag. Use tip no. 1A.
- Start on the outer edges and work your way towards the middle in circles. Finish with a peak on top.
- Sprinkle Daim/Skor pieces over the frosting.
- Top off with colored sprinkles.
- Lastly, add the decorative candles.

> *Tip*
> The Daim cupcakes taste great with a side of vanilla ice cream.

AUNT GERD'S FLOWER MEADOW CUPCAKES

My aunt Gerd is a master in the kitchen, and she always whisks up the most delicious cakes for our family gatherings. This lemon recipe from Gerd's kitchen is one of our absolute favorites and we wish to share it with you. Here we have chosen a meadow as a theme to show how cupcakes can decorate a table just as efficiently as flowers.

{18 CUPCAKES}

You need:

THE BATTER

3 eggs
⅔ cup (150 g) margarine
2 ⅓ cups (300 g) white
    all-purpose flour
1 ½ cups (300 g) sugar
2 tbsp baking powder
1 cup (⅓ liter) milk
grated zest on 1 lemon
the juice of ½ lemon

THE FROSTING

4 oz or ½ cup (125 g)
    cream cheese
½ stick (60 g) margarine
3 to 3 ⅓ cups (354 to 405 g)
    powdered sugar
2 tsp vanilla sugar
3 ⅓ tbsp (200 ml) lemon
    juice

Preparation:

- Preheat the oven to 350°F/175°C.
- Place 18 muffin cups in a muffin pan.
- Whisk the margarine and sugar white.
- Add the eggs, one at a time, and whisk well between each egg.
- Add lemon, flour, and baking powder.
- Pour in the milk, and stir well.
- Fill the muffin cups half full.
- Bake the cakes in the middle of the oven for about 15 minutes.
- Remove them form the oven and let them cool for about 5 minutes in the pan. Move them onto a cooling rack, and allow them to cool completely.

THE FROSTING

- Whisk all of the ingredients together into a light cream.

DECORATING

- Place the frosting in a decorating bag. Use tip no. 1M.
- Buy flower decorations, or you can make flowers on your own with fondant.
- Add food coloring if desired.

Tip

An alternate décor with a lovely taste is caramelized lemon zest: Fold lemon zest in thin shreds in melted sugar in a pan. When they have cooled completely add them on top of the frosting.

SWEET RASPBERRY CUPCAKES

These sweet raspberry cupcakes have a fresh and lovely taste of summer. They are perfect for solstice and gatherings around the bonfire when it is getting close to midnight.

{20 CUPCAKES}

You need:

THE BATTER
4 eggs
1 ¼ cups (250 g) sugar
2 cups (264 g) white all-purpose flour
2 tsp baking powder
3 tsp vanilla extract
1 ¼ cups (2.1 fl oz) whipping cream
1 ¾ sticks (200 g) margarine
1 packet of raspberry Jell-O powder
fresh raspberries

THE FROSTING
2 cups (250 g) powdered sugar
1 cup (250 g) margarine, room temperature
1 tsp vanilla extract
½ cup (122 g) raspberry puree*

*RASPBERRY PUREE
Warm fresh raspberries in a saucepan. Add about 2 tbsp of sugar and the juice of ½ lemon. Stir well. Sift the puree to remove the small, bitter, raspberry seeds.

Preparation:

- Preheat the oven to 390°F/200°C.
- Place 20 muffin cups in a muffin pan.
- Whisk eggs and sugar until stiff and fluffy.
- Add melted margarine, baking powder, flour, and vanilla sugar. Stir well.
- Add the raspberry Jell-O powder and whipping cream and whisk the batter until all the lumps are gone.
- Place 2 to 3 fresh raspberries in each muffin cup.
- Fill the muffin cups half full.
- Bake the cakes in the middle of the oven for about 15 minutes.
- Remove them from the oven and cool them in the muffin pan for about 5 minutes. Move them onto a cooling rack, and let them cool completely.

THE FROSTING
- Whisk all of the ingredients with a mixer on low speed until everything is blended together. Increase the speed and whisk on high speed for 2 to 3 minutes more.

DECORATING
- Place the frosting in a decorating bag. Use tip no. 2D to make small florets. Squeeze until the florets have the preferred size and then repeat. Start on the inside of the previous floret. Continue until the entire cupcake is covered.
- Decorate with fresh raspberries or serve raspberries on the side.

Tip
The raspberry puree needs to be completely cool; if not the frosting will melt.

SOCCER CUPCAKES (GLUTEN FREE)

Cupcakes are for everyone—even for those with a gluten allergy. Everyone can look forward to these cupcakes with their delicious vanilla taste. Here we have chosen a soccer theme to show how cupcakes can be desirable for the tough boys as well.

{24 CUPCAKES}

You need:

THE BATTER
4 eggs
1 ⅔ cups (338 g) sugar
1 cup (250 g) margarine, room temperature
1 cup (⅕ liter) milk
3 tbsp baking powder
2 ½ cups (405 g) gluten-free flour
1 ½ tsp vanilla extract

FROSTING
1 cup (250 g) margarine
2 tsp vanilla extract
⅓ cup (100 ml) milk
5 to 6 ¾ cups (608 to 810 g) powdered sugar

The gluten-free flour makes the cupcakes somewhat drier than regular flour. In other words, these cupcakes will not be as moist as the others in this book.

Preparation:

- Preheat the oven to 350°F/175°C.
- Place 24 muffin cups in a muffin pan.
- Stir margarine and sugar white. Whisk until soft and airy.
- Whisk in the eggs, one at a time.
- Add the milk, flour, and baking powder alternately.
- Add the vanilla extract.
- Fill the muffin cups half full
- Bake the cakes in the middle of the oven for about 20 minutes.
- Remove them from the oven and cool in the pan for about 5 minutes. Move them onto a cooling rack, and let them cool completely.

THE FROSTING
- Whisk the margarine airy.
- Add the vanilla extract.
- Alternate between adding sifted powdered sugar and milk. Add powdered sugar until the mixture has a soft and creamy texture.
- Add the green food coloring.

DECORATING
- Place the frosting in a decorating bag. Use tip no. 233.
- Squeeze the grass as tight-knit as possible. You shouldn't be able to see the cupcake at all.
- Use soccer décor from any decoration store. Alternately, you may buy soccer balls made of icing to place on the grass mat.

Tip
If you want your favorite players or favorite team on the cupcakes, you can order sugar slices with their pictures on them from various online sources.

A TASTE OF HONEY CUPCAKES

My grandfather once had beehives in his yard and would enjoy the honey. Granted, I would get my fair share of enjoyment out of it as well. The natural sweetness in the honey makes it great for cupcakes. These are moist and taste like summer and sunshine.

{12 CUPCAKES}

You need:

THE BATTER

2 eggs
⅔ cup (150 g) margarine, room temperature
½ cup (100 g) sugar
2 tbsp honey
1 ⅓ cups (150 g) white all-purpose flour
2 ½ tsp baking powder

FROSTING

⅔ cup (150 g) margarine, room temperature
2 ½ to 3 cups (300 to 354 g) powdered sugar
1 tsp vanilla extract
1 tsp orange food coloring
2 to 3 tbsp honey (for flavor)
1 to 2 tbsp freshly-squeezed lemon juice

Preparation:

- Preheat the oven to 360°F/180°C.
- Place 12 muffin cups in a muffin pan.
- Whisk margarine, sugar, and honey until light and creamy.
- Whisk in the eggs, one at a time.
- Fold in sifted flour and baking powder. Mix well.
- Fill the muffin cups half full.
- Bake the cupcakes in the oven for 10 to 15 minutes.
- Remove them from the oven and cool them in the muffin pan for about 5 minutes. Move them onto a cooling rack, and let them cool completely.

THE FROSTING

- Blend all of the ingredients, excluding the honey and food coloring.
- Flavor with the preferred amount of honey.
- Use orange or yellow food coloring for a yellowish color.

DECORATING

- Use a decorating bag and tip no. 1M.
- Start at the edges and work the tip inwards.
- Make ladybugs and bees out of marzipan or colored fondant.
- Use a black food marker to create the details.
- Make fondant or marzipan flowers in various sizes and colors.

Tip
There are many varieties of honey, but use one with a medium strength in taste.

"IT'S A GIRL!" CUPCAKES

Bring these cupcakes the next time you attend a baby shower for a close friend. The baby pink champagne cupcakes are delicate, cute, and adorable, and they are great as a gift for the new mom.

{12 CUPCAKES}

You need:

THE BATTER
2 eggs
¾ cup (150 g) sugar
1 stick (125 g) margarine
2 tsp vanilla extract
½ cup (1.7 fl oz) heavy whipping cream
1 ¼ cups (158 g) white all-purpose flour
1 tsp baking powder
½ cup (3.5 fl oz) sweet pink champagne

THE FROSTING
1 stick (125 g) margarine
1 tsp vanilla extract
about 2 ½ cups (300 g) powdered sugar
2 to 3 tbsp champagne*
light pink food coloring

*You need a tad bit more powdered sugar in the frosting when you add champagne. The frosting should be firm and spreadable. Instead of champagne you can use 2 to 3 tbsp whipping cream if you prefer.

Preparation:

- Preheat the oven to 350°F/175°C.
- Place 12 muffin cups in a muffin pan.
- Stir the margarine and the sugar until white.
- Add the eggs, and stir well.
- Sift the flour and baking powder in the bowl, while also adding the champagne in segments.
- Add the vanilla extract.
- Pour in the whipping cream and whisk everything for 1 to 2 minutes.
- Fill the muffin cups half full.
- Bake the cakes for about 20 minutes.
- Remove them from the oven and cool them in the pan for about 5 minutes. Move them onto a cooling rack, and let them cool completely.

THE FROSTING
- Whisk margarine, powdered sugar, vanilla extract, and champagne.
- Add the pink food coloring.

DECORATING
- Place the frosting in a decorating bag. Use tip no. 2D.
- Squeeze a thick layer of frosting on the cupcakes. Start at the edge and move inwards in circles. The shape of the tip will give the cupcake a peaked look.
- Use cookie cutters to make flowers. Feel free to decorate with a sugar diamond in the middle of the flower for a luxurious look.
- Sprinkle glitter dust on top before you serve.

Tip
If it's a boy, replace the pink muffin cups with light blue, and use light blue decorations.

MOJITO CUPCAKES

The Mojito is not just a popular drink! The wonderfully fresh mint leaves give these cupcakes a lovely taste of summer and are suitable for most occasions. If you prefer not to use alcohol, you may substitute lemon juice for the rum.

{12 CUPCAKES}

You need:

THE BATTER
4 eggs
2 cups (422 g) sugar
1 cup (¼ liter) skim sour milk
1 tbsp rum (Captain Morgan spiced rum is best)
1 tsp vanilla extract
3 cups (396 g) white all-purpose flour
1 tsp baking powder
½ tsp baking soda
1 tsp salt
1 cup (250 g) margarine, room temperature

THE RUM SYRUP
1 cup (210 g) sugar
¼ cup (1.75 fl oz) water
½ stick (60 g) margarine
¼ cup (1.75 fl oz) rum
grated zest of 1 lime
8 to 10 mint leaves

FROSTING
8 oz or 1 cup (225 g) cream cheese
2 cups (250 g) powdered sugar
1 tbsp lime juice, freshly squeezed
a few drops green food coloring

Preparation:

- Preheat the oven to 335°F/170°C.
- Place 12 muffin cups in a muffin pan.
- Blend skim milk, vanilla extract, and rum in a bowl.
- In a separate bowl, blend sifted flour, baking powder, baking soda, and salt.
- Whisk margarine and sugar until white.
- Fold in the eggs, one at a time, whisking well between each egg.
- Alternate between adding the sifted flour mixture and the milk mixture to the margarine mixture.
- Whip on medium speed for about 3 minutes until the ingredients are blended together.
- Fill the muffin cups two-thirds full.
- Bake the cakes in the middle of the oven for about 25 minutes.
- Remove them from the oven and cool the in the muffin pan for about 5 minutes.

THE RUM SYRUP
- Bring sugar, water, and margarine to a boil while stirring.
- Cool but keep stirring so nothing sticks to the bottom.
- Wait until the blend is completely cool before you add the rum, grated lime zests, and mint leaves. (The leaves are only for flavor; they are not going to be eaten.)
- While the cupcakes are still lukewarm, dunk them into the syrup. Use a tablespoon. Feel free to poke small holes in the top of the cupcakes to make it easier to absorb the liquid.
- Cool the cupcakes completely before you decorate with the frosting.

THE FROSTING
- Whisk cream cheese, sifted powdered sugar, freshly squeezed lime juice, and a few drops of food coloring together.

DECORATING
- Place the frosting in a decorating bag. Use tip no. 4B.
- Be generous with the cream.
- Decorate with fresh mint leafs and a small slice of lime.

COOKIE CUPCAKES

Oreo cookies are so tasty. The combination of chocolate, vanilla, and cookie is fantastic in a cupcake!

{16 CUPCAKES}

You need:

THE BATTER
2 eggs
½ cup (90 g) margarine, room temperature
1 cup (200 g) brown sugar
4.5 oz (125 g) dark chocolate
2 tsp vanilla extract
1 cup (150 g) flour
1 tsp baking powder
½ tsp baking soda
4 crushed Oreo cookies
1 cup (⅕ liter) milk

THE FROSTING
⅔ cup (150 g) margarine, room temperature
3 ¾ cups (450 g) powdered sugar
about ¼ cup (3 ½ tbsp) milk
½ tsp vanilla extract
6 crushed Oreo cookies

Preparation:

- Preheat the oven to 360°F/180°C.
- Place 6 muffin cups in a muffin pan.
- Melt the chocolate in a water bath or in the microwave.
- Whisk margarine and sugar.
- Add the eggs, one at a time. Whisk well between each egg.
- Add the chocolate and vanilla. Continue to stir well.
- Add sifted flour, baking powder, and baking soda. Alternate by adding the milk as well.
- Crush the Oreo cookies in a plastic bag. You may use a rolling pin or something similar to carefully thump the bag.
- Mix the crushed cookies in with the batter.
- Fill the muffin cups two-thirds full.
- Bake the cakes at the middle of the oven for about 20 minutes.
- Remove them from the oven and cool them in the pan for about 5 minutes. Move them onto a cooling rack, and let them cool completely.

THE FROSTING
- Whip margarine and powdered sugar.
- Add vanilla extract and milk.
- Fold in crushed Oreo cookies. The Oreos should be finely crushed, so that you may easily squeeze them through the tip of the decorating bag.

DECORATING
- Place the frosting in a decorating bag. Use tip no. 6B.
- Start in the middle and work your way to the outer edge of the cupcakes in circular movements. Try to squeeze the bag evenly throughout.
- Divide Oreo cookies in two down the middle. Use a sharp knife and cut quickly so that the cookie doesn't crack.
- Decorate each cupcake with half an Oreo cookie.

STRAWBERRY AND CHAMPAGNE CUPCAKES

Why not serve cupcakes with strawberries and champagne to spark that romantic flame? With fresh, organic strawberries, these cupcakes are to die for! This recipe gives quite a large batch so feel free to cut it in half if it's only you and your man (or woman).

{28 CUPCAKES}

You need:

THE BATTER
¾ cup (175 g) margarine, room temperature
1 ½ cups (294 g) sugar
6 egg whites
3 cups (370 g) white all-purpose flour
2 cups (15.8 fl oz) champagne
3 tsp baking powder
10 strawberries

FROSTING
1 cup (225 g) margarine, room temperature
2 tbsp whipping cream
1 tsp vanilla extract
2 ½ to 3 ⅓ cups (300 to 405 g) powdered sugar
15 strawberries (for decorating)

Preparation:

- Preheat the oven to 350°F/175°C.
- Place 28 cupcake baking cups on three baking sheets.
- Whisk margarine and sugar until white.
- Add sifted flour and baking powder in batches, while adding the champagne in between.
- Whisk the egg white until white and foaming. Add to the batter.
- Fold in diced strawberries. Carefully stir.
- Fill the cupcake cups half full.
- Bake the cakes in the oven for 17 to 20 minutes.
- Take them out and cool on the sheet for about 5 minutes. Move them onto a cooling rack, and let them cool completely.

FROSTING
- Stir margarine, cream, and vanilla extract together.
- Sift the powdered sugar in the bowl, a little at a time.

DECORATING
- Place the frosting in a decorating bag. Use tip number 1M.
- Start on the outer edges and work your way to the top of the cupcake in circular movements.
- Cut the strawberries in quarters, and place them on top of the frosting with the sliced side pointing upwards. You may also sprinkle some edible glitter or chopped pistachios on top.

COOKIE MONSTER CUPCAKES

Kids love funny-looking cupcakes, and for birthdays it is especially exciting to make something out of the ordinary. Here is the cookie monster.

{24 CUPCAKES}

You need:

THE BATTER

8 eggs

2 cups (422 g) sugar

1 ½ cups (350 g) margarine, room temperature

3 cups (396 g) all-purpose flour, sifted

1 cup (¼ liter) coconut milk

2 tsp baking powder

1 tsp salt

½ tsp vanilla extract

1 ¼ cups (117 g) grated coconut

THE FROSTING

5 ⅓ cups (625 g) powdered sugar

1 cup (185 g) margarine, room temperature

5 to 6 tbsp coconut milk

colored grated coconut for decorating*

12 chocolate chip cookies

*Mix the grated coconut with food coloring to obtain the right color for the cookie monster.

Preparation:

- Preheat the oven to 350°F/175°C.
- Place 24 muffin cups in a muffin pan.
- Whisk the margarine and sugar until white.
- Separate the yolks and egg whites.
- Add the yolks to the mixture, one at a time.
- Add salt, baking powder, and vanilla extract.
- Add sifted flour and coconut milk alternately. Stir well.
- In a separate bowl, whisk the egg whites until stiff. Whisk on medium speed for 3 minutes.
- Blend the grated coconut and egg whites. Fold in with the rest of the batter.
- Fill the muffin cups two-thirds full.
- Bake the cakes in the middle of the oven for about 20 minutes.
- Remove them from the oven and let them cool in the pan for about 5 minutes. Move them onto a cooling rack, and let them cool completely.

THE FROSTING

- Place the margarine and powdered sugar in a bowl. Add the coconut milk and whisk on low speed. Increase the speed of the mixer once the ingredients have blended. Whisk for about 5 minutes total.

DECORATING

- Use a spatula to spread the frosting on the cupcakes.
- Spread it evenly.
- Dip the cupcakes in a bowl of grated coconut. Make sure that the coconut is evenly distributed over the whole cupcake.
- Decorate with eyes from a cake store. You may alternatively make eyes yourself by rolling out two fondant marbles and drawing on black pupils with a black food marker.
- Place a chocolate chip cookie in the mouth of each cookie monster.

CHEESECAKE CUPCAKES

Cheesecake is the favorite of many, despite the fact that it is quite filling. Now you can finally serve this favorite in a cupcake size. The same good flavor remains, and we use the same ingredients, just a tad bit less of the good! The result is best when the cupcakes are baked in silicone cups.

{12 CUPCAKES}

You need:

THE BATTER

3 eggs
4.5 oz (125 g) graham crackers
2 tsp vanilla sauce
1 ⅓ cups (175 g) powdered sugar
5 tbsp margarine, room temperature
16 oz or 2 cups (450 g) cream cheese
16 oz (450 g) ricotta cheese
12 fresh strawberries

Preparation:

- Preheat the oven to 320°F/160°C.
- Place 12 muffin cups in a muffin pan.
- Crush the graham crackers in a bowl. Blend the margarine with the crackers to create a firm cracker mass.
- Press the mixture into the bottom of the muffin cups.
- Place the cups in the fridge so that the bottoms stiffen.
- Whisk the ricotta cheese until soft and spreadable. Fold in the vanilla sauce and cream cheese. Sift in the powdered sugar. Mix everything together.
- Add the eggs, one at a time. Whisk well between each egg.
- Fill the muffin cups two-thirds full.
- Bake the cakes in the middle of the oven for about 25 minutes.
- Remove them from the oven and cool them in the pan for about 5 minutes. Then place them in the fridge, and let them cool completely.
- Keep the cupcakes in the fridge until serving.

DECORATING

- Right before serving, decorate the cupcakes with shreds of fresh strawberries. Shred the berries with a very sharp knife.

MERINGUE CUPCAKES

Lemon meringue tastes wonderfully sweet and fresh. The taste is unbeatable in cupcakes. These cupcakes are good for any occasion—you can even bring them along to your next picnic. I promise that these will be a success and no one will be able to resist.

{14 CUPCAKES}

You need:

THE BATTER
4 eggs
1 cup (190 g) sugar
1 cup (225 g) margarine,
  room temperature
1 ½ cups (200 g) all-purpose
  flour
4 tsp baking powder
1 tsp vanilla extract

LEMON BUTTER
1 cup (200 g) sugar
⅓ cup (40 g) cornstarch
¼ tsp salt
3 tbsp margarine, room
  temperature
⅔ cup (5.3 fl oz) warm water
3 egg yolks
4 tbsp freshly-squeezed
  lemon juice
zest of 1 lemon

MERINGUE
3 egg whites
⅓ cup (65 g) sugar
½ tsp cream of tartar

Tip
You can find cream of tartar at your grocery store.

Preparation:

- Preheat the oven to 350°F/175°C.
- Place 14 muffin cups in a muffin pan.
- Whisk all of the ingredients for the batter together. Whisk the batter until even.
- Fill the muffin cups two-thirds full.
- Bake the cakes in the middle of the oven for about 20 minutes.
- Remove them from the oven and cool them in the muffin pan for about 5 minutes. Move them onto a cooling rack, and let them cool completely.

THE LEMON BUTTER
- Add sugar, cornstarch, and salt in a bowl that can withstand heat and mix well. The bowl is now going to stand in a water bath so fill a frying pan about two-thirds full with water. Warm the water to 168°F/75°C—it should not be boiling.
- Add the warm water to the mixture, a little at the time, and mix well.
- Add grated lemon zest, lemon juice, margarine, and yolks. Constantly stir and increase the temperature of the water bath until it is almost boiling. Continue stirring until the butter thickens. Cover with parchment paper, and let it cool to room temperature.

MERINGUE
- Set the oven to 450°F/230°C.
- Whisk the eggs and cream of tartar for about 2 minutes.
- Add sugar, a little at a time, and whisk well in between.
- When the mass is stiff and airy, scoop it into a decorating bag. Squeeze the meringue out on top of the cool cupcakes. Place the cupcakes back in the oven and bake them for about 5 minutes. The meringue should become golden brown.
- Remove the cupcakes from the oven. Place them on a cooling rack and let them cool.
- Cut the cupcakes in half and fill with lemon butter between the layers.

PASSION FRUIT CUPCAKES

Vanilla and citrus fruits are classic flavors in the world of cupcakes. Passion fruit is an exotic and fresh fruit that will both surprise and give joy to many.

{12 CUPCAKES}

You need:

THE BATTER:

2 eggs
⅓ cup (75 g) margarine, room temperature
½ cup (120 g) sugar
1 tsp baking powder
1 ¼ cups (160 g) white all-purpose flour
5 passion fruits
1 tsp vanilla extract

THE FROSTING

3 cups (354 g) powdered sugar
6 oz or ¾ cup (150 g) cream cheese, room temperature
½ stick (60 g) margarine, room temperature
2 passion fruits

Preparation:

- Preheat the oven to 360°F/180°C.
- Place 12 muffin cups in a muffin pan.
- Scrape the fruit pulp out of the passion fruits and pass through a sieve to remove the seeds. Use the backside of a spoon to push it through. If you find it hard to make the juice separate from the seeds, first place the fruit in the microwave for a couple of seconds. You'll need about 3 ⅓ tbsp (50 ml) of passion fruit juice.
- Whisk margarine, sugar, and eggs.
- Sift the flour and baking powder in the bowl, and add the vanilla extract. Stir well.
- Add the passion fruit juice.
- Fill the muffin cups two-thirds full.
- Bake the cakes in the middle of the oven for 17 to 20 minutes.
- Remove them from the oven, and cool them in the pan for about 5 minutes. Move the cupcakes onto a cooling rack, and let them cool completely.

THE FROSTING

- Whisk cream cheese, margarine, powdered sugar, and passion fruit juice until the frosting is soft and spreadable.

DECORATING

- Place the frosting in a decorating bag. Use tip no. 1M.
- Finally, if you want an extra-fresh experience of the sweet and tart, pour the passion fruit juice with seeds over the cupcakes.

PATTY CAKES

Here's the recipe for one of the very first varieties of cupcakes ever made! My mother saved this recipe from when she attended a home education class in New Zealand during the 1960s. Patty cakes are basically the foundation for cupcakes.

{12 CUPCAKES}

You need:

THE BATTER
2 eggs
½ cup (120 g) margarine, melted
½ cup (120 g) sugar
⅓ cup (5 tbsp) milk
2 ⅓ cups (300 g) white all-purpose flour
2 tsp baking powder
barely ½ tsp salt

THE FROSTING
1 ¼ cups (152 g) powdered sugar
1 ½ tsp margarine, room temperature
red food coloring / raspberry extract
3 tbsp warm water

Preparation:

- Preheat the oven to 390°F/200°C.
- Place 12 muffin cups in a muffin pan.
- Whisk eggs and sugar until white.
- Add melted margarine.
- Stir in the flour with salt and baking powder.
- Add the milk, and whisk well.
- Fill the muffin cups two-thirds full.
- Bake the cakes in the middle of the oven for about 10 to 15 minutes.
- Remove them from the oven, and cool them in the pan for about 5 minutes. Move them onto a cooling rack, and let them cool completely.

THE FROSTING
- Stir powdered sugar, margarine, food coloring, and water together in a bowl.
- This frosting should not have the texture of buttercream. Rather, it should be more liquid-like or spreadable and light.

DECORATING
- Use a spoon to cover the cupcakes with the frosting. Use a spatula to make an even surface.
- Decorate with sprinkles if wanted.

Tip
These cupcakes are delicious even without the frosting!

PIÑA COLADA CUPCAKES

The piña colada cupcakes are the perfect party treats. The exotic pineapple and coconut drink is transformed into a tasty finger food— lovely for both the eyes and the palate.

{12 CUPCAKES.}

You need:

THE BATTER
2 eggs
1 cup (131 g) white all-purpose flour
2 tsp baking powder
½ tsp salt
1 cup (175 g) sugar
3 tbsp sunflower oil
3 to 6 rings canned pineapple, dried with a paper towel
1 ½ cups (⅓ liter) coconut milk
Malibu rum, for flavoring
2 tsp vanilla extract

THE FROSTING
8.8 oz, or a little over 1 cup (250 g) cream cheese
⅓ cup (75 g) margarine, room temperature
6 tsp Malibu rum
1 cup (215 g) coconut milk powder
2 ⅔ cups (315 g) powdered sugar

Preparation:

- Preheat the oven to 350°F/175°C.
- Place 12 muffin cups in a muffin pan.
- Blend flour, baking powder, and salt in a bowl.
- In a separate bowl, blend rum and coconut milk.
- Whisk sugar and oil in a mixer.
- Add the eggs, one at a time.
- Add the flour and coconut milk mixture, and whisk everything for about 3 minutes on medium speed.
- Add the vanilla extract and pineapple. Carefully stir but do not break the pineapple pieces.
- Use a large spoon or an ice-cream scoop to scoop the batter into the muffin cups. Fill them two-thirds full.
- Bake the cakes in the middle of the oven for 18 to 20 minutes.
- Remove them from the oven, and let them cool in the pan for 5 minutes. Then move them onto a cooling rack to cool completely.

THE FROSTING
- Whisk cream cheese, margarine, Malibu rum, coconut milk powder, and powdered sugar with a mixer on medium speed for about 5 minutes.

DECORATING
- Place the frosting in a decorating bag. Use tip no. 8B.
- If you want there to be a variety of color on the frosting, just divide the frosting into multiple bowls before coloring.
- Decorate with umbrellas and colorful straws.

RED VELVET CUPCAKES

Valentine's Day is basically made for cupcakes. In the United States, the deep-red red velvet cupcakes have been a long-standing favorite on the day of love. Let the taste seduce you!

{12 CUPCAKES.}

You need:

THE BATTER
1 egg
½ stick (60 g) margarine
¾ cup (150 g) sugar
½ tsp vanilla extract
½ tsp vinegar
½ tsp baking soda
½ cup (8 tbsp) sour milk
1 cup (125 g) white all-purpose flour
1 tbsp cocoa powder
a few drops of deep red food color

THE FROSTING
6 oz or ⅔ cup (150 g) cream cheese
⅔ cup (150 g) margarine, room temperature
3.5 oz, or a little over ½ cup (100 g) white chocolate
2 cups (250 g) powdered sugar

Preparation:

- Preheat the oven to 350°F/175°C.
- Place 12 muffin cups in a muffin pan
- Whisk eggs and sugar until stiff.
- Add margarine and vanilla extract.
- In a separate bowl, blend baking soda and vinegar before adding it to the batter.
- Add the sour milk, cocoa powder, and flour. Whisk until the batter obtains a creamy texture.
- Add the food coloring.
- Fill the muffin cups two-thirds full.
- Bake the cakes in the middle of the oven for 18 to 20 minutes.
- Remove them from the oven, and cool in the pan for about 5 minutes. Move them onto a cooling rack, and let them cool completely.

THE FROSTING
- Melt the chocolate in the microwave or in a water bath.
- While the chocolate cools, whisk margarine and cream cheese.
- Add the powdered sugar and chocolate alternately. Make sure that the chocolate is completely cool.
- Whisk into a creamy texture.
- If the frosting is not stiff enough, you can add more powdered sugar.

DECORATING
- Place the frosting in a decorating bag. Use tip no. 1M.
- Start on the outer edge and move inwards towards the middle of the cake in circular movements.
- Sprinkle heart-shaped sprinkles on top.

Tip
With regular red food coloring from the grocery store, you'll need about 2 tbsp (30 ml) of color. If you use a paste from Wilton, you'll need about 1 tbsp of color.

SEXY CHOCOLATE CUPCAKES

Every day is a golden opportunity to treat your boyfriend or girlfriend to some extra attention. Traditionally, boxed chocolates have been the gift of choice. Cupcakes with chocolates are not a bad way to go either. These have a full chocolate taste and may be decorated as romantically as you want. Why not "say it" with cupcakes instead of a card?

{12 CUPCAKES}

You need:

THE BATTER
4 eggs
⅗ cup (125 g) sugar
1 ¾ sticks (200 g) margarine
8 oz (225 g) dark chocolate pieces
⅝ cup (100 g) white all-purpose flour
1 tsp baking powder
2 tbsp chocolate sauce

THE FROSTING
½ cup (100 g) margarine, room temperature
3 cups (350 g) powdered sugar
barely ⅓ cup (3 ½ tbsp) whole milk
3 tbsp + 1 tsp (4 tbsp) chocolate sauce
⅔ cup (40 g) cocoa powder

Preparation:

- Preheat the oven to 350°F/175°C.
- Place 12 muffin cups in a muffin pan.
- Melt the margarine and chocolate pieces in a saucepan or the microwave.
- Stir well and let the blend cool.
- Whisk eggs and sugar until stiff.
- Fold in flour and baking powder.
- Add the chocolate and butter blend and the chocolate sauce. Whisk until the batter is even and without lumps.
- Fill the muffin cups two-thirds full.
- Bake the cakes in the middle of the oven for about 20 minutes.
- Remove them from the oven, and cool them in the pan for about 5 minutes. Move them onto a cooling rack, and let them cool completely.

THE FROSTING
- Whisk the margarine, powdered sugar, chocolate sauce, and cocoa powder together with a mixer on low speed.
- Add milk, a little at a time, and whisk well in between.
- Lastly, whisk for 3 to 4 minutes on high speed to create the right fluffy texture.

DECORATING
- Place the frosting in a decorating bag. Use tip no. 2F.
- Use marzipan or fondant, colored red, and a heart-shaped cutter.

Tip
Instead of chocolate frosting, you can serve these cupcakes with chocolate or vanilla ice cream on top. A fantastic combination!

LEMON CUPCAKES WITH POPPY SEEDS

Lemon creates a delightfully fresh taste in cupcakes. These are as fresh as they look!

{12 CUPCAKES}

You need:

THE BATTER
4 eggs
1 cup (225 g) margarine, room temperature
1 cup (190 g) sugar
1 ½ cups (200 g) white all-purpose flour
2 ½ tsp baking powder
1 tsp vanilla extract
1 tbsp poppy seeds
1 tbsp grated lemon zest

THE FROSTING
2 cups (250 g) powdered sugar
8 tbsp lemon juice
2 to 3 tbsp poppy seeds

Preparation:

- Preheat the oven to 350°F/175°C.
- Place 12 muffin cups in a muffin pan.
- Whisk margarine, sugar, flour, baking powder, and eggs together in a bowl.
- Add the vanilla extract, poppy seeds, and lemon zest. Whisk well for 3 to 4 minutes.
- Fill the muffin cups about half full.
- Bake the cakes in the middle of the oven for about 20 minutes.
- Remove them from the oven, and cool them in the muffin pan for about 5 minutes. Move them onto a cooling rack, and let them cool completely.

THE FROSTING
- Mix everything in a bowl and stir well.

DECORATING
- Use a spoon to scoop the frosting on top of the cupcakes, letting the frosting run all over the cupcakes so that it is completely covered.
- Decorate with poppy seeds or other preferred decoration.

PRINCESS CUPCAKES

There lives a small princess in every little girl, and real princess cupcakes are usually very popular as a birthday treat. The white chocolate frosting will be a hit with the bigger princesses as well—and princes. Guaranteed!

{18 CUPCAKES}

You need:

THE BATTER

2 eggs
1 cup (210 g) sugar
½ cup (115 g) margarine, room temperature
½ cup (45 g) cocoa powder
1 cup (¼ liter) warm coffee
1 ¼ cups (158 g) white all-purpose flour
1 tsp baking soda
¼ tsp baking powder
1 pinch of salt
3.5 oz, or a little over ½ cup (100 g) milk chocolate

THE FROSTING

1 cup (225 g) margarine, room temperature
8 oz or 1 cup (225 g) cream cheese
4 oz or ⅔ cup (115 g) white chocolate
2 to 2 ½ cups (250 to 300 g) powdered sugar
pink food coloring

Preparation:

- Preheat the oven to 350°F/175°C.
- Place 18 muffin cups in the muffin pan.
- Whisk margarine and sugar in a bowl.
- Add eggs and whisk into a fluffy buttercream.
- Stir in the black coffee and sifted cocoa powder. Cool the cream.
- In a separate bowl, sift the flour and baking powder, baking soda, and salt. Blend well.
- Stir the dry ingredients in with the coffee and cocoa blend, a little at a time. Stir well.
- Turn the chocolate pieces in with the batter.
- Fill the muffin cups two-thirds full.
- Bake the cakes in the oven for about 18 minutes.
- Remove them from the oven, and cool them in the pan for about 5 minutes. Move the cupcakes onto a cooling rack, and let them cool completely.

THE FROSTING

- Whisk the margarine and cream cheese together.
- Sift the powdered sugar in the bowl, and whisk well.
- Melt the chocolate in a water bath or in the microwave. Let it cool.
- Stir in the melted chocolate.
- Add food coloring if desired.

DECORATING

- Place the frosting in a decorating bag. Use tip no. 1M.
- Decorate with pink crown candles from a party store.

Tip
Let the cream cheese maintain a fridge temperature, and the frosting will be easier to work with.

WILD BERRY CUPCAKES

Berries and cupcakes simply belong together. Raspberries and blueberries are a few of my absolute favorites from nature's pantry—healthy, fresh, and natural.

{12 CUPCAKES}

You need:

THE BATTER
1 egg
¾ cup (150 g) sugar
1 cup (125 g) white
   all-purpose flour
½ tsp vanilla extract
½ stick (60 g) margarine,
   room temperature
½ tsp baking soda
½ tsp vinegar
⅔ cup (148 ml) sour milk
1 ⅓ cups (200 g) fresh blueberries and raspberries

THE FROSTING
3 to 3 ⅓ cups (354 to 405 g)
   powdered sugar
1 stick (125 g) margarine,
   room temperature
3 ½ tbsp milk
1 tsp vanilla extract
2 to 3 tsp lemon juice
food coloring if wanted

Preparation:

- Preheat the oven to 350°F/175°C.
- Place 12 muffin cups in a muffin pan.
- Blend baking soda and vinegar in a bowl. In a separate bowl whisk sugar and eggs until fluffy.
- Stir in the margarine and vanilla extract.
- Fold in the vinegar and baking soda blend.
- Add the sour milk and flour alternately.
- Turn in the berries.
- Fill the muffin cups two-thirds full.
- Bake the cakes in the oven for about 20 minutes.
- Remove them from the oven, and cool them for about 5 minutes. Move the cupcakes onto a cooling rack, and let them cool completely.

THE FROSTING
- Stir margarine, milk, lemon juice (for flavor), and vanilla extract together.
- Sift the powdered sugar into the bowl. The frosting should have a firm texture.

DECORATING
- Place the frosting in a decorating bag. Use tip no. 1M.
- Decorate with fresh red currants, blueberries, and strawberries.

Tip
Add 3 tbsp of cocoa powder or 4 tbsp chocolate sauce to the batter if you want the cupcakes to be chocolate flavored.

DARK CHOCOLATE CUPCAKES

Many shy away from cupcakes because they worry about the calories. But if you are active and on the go, and need a small snack, this cupcake made with dark chocolate is a great alternative that you don't need to feel bad about eating. Enjoy these!

{12 CUPCAKES}

You Need:

THE BATTER

1 egg

3 egg whites

½ cup (100 g) natural sweetener

⅔ cup (150 g) brown sugar

3 tbsp white all-purpose flour

1 pinch of salt

1 tsp vanilla extract

½ cup (50 g) cocoa powder

¾ cup (177 ml) skim milk

4 oz (115 g) dark chocolate, minimum 70% cocoa

¼ tsp lemon juice

1 tsp orange extract

Preparation:

• Warm the vanilla extract, salt, milk, orange extract, flour, sugar, sweetener, and cocoa powder in a pot on medium heat. Warm until the sugar has dissolved.

• Add the chocolate and stir until melted. Remove the pot from the stove.

• Empty the mixture into a bowl. Add the eggs, and whisk well.

• Set the batter aside, and let it cool.

• Whisk egg whites and lemon juice. Whisk for about 5 minutes with a mixer on high speed.

• Fold the stiff egg whites in with the chocolate mixture. Whisk on medium speed until the batter is even.

• Fill the baking cups halfway.

• Bake the cakes in the middle of the oven for about 20 minutes.

• Remove them from the oven, and cool them in the baking sheet for about 5 minutes. Place the cupcakes on a cooling rack, and let them cool completely.

FROSTING

• Sift some cocoa powder or powdered sugar on top.

• If you want to create a decorative pattern, you can use a stencil. For instance, you may cut a small heart out of paper and place it on the cupcake before you cover it with the cocoa or powdered sugar. You may also buy stencils in certain specialty stores.

VANILLA CUPCAKES INSPIRED BY MAGNOLIA BAKERY

Magnolia Bakery is a cupcake bakery that became famous on the TV show *Sex and the City*. Here's a recipe reminiscent of the heavenly vanilla cupcakes that's on everyone's lips.

{24 CUPCAKES}

You need:

THE BATTER

4 eggs
1 ⅔ cups (338 g) sugar
1 cup (250 g) margarine, room temperature
1 cup (⅕ liter) milk
3 tsp baking powder
2 ½ cups (316 g) white all-purpose flour
2 tsp vanilla extract

THE FROSTING

1 cup (250 g) margarine, room temperature
2 tsp vanilla extract
½ cup (100 ml) milk
5 to 6 ¾ cups (608 to 810 g) powdered sugar
2 tsp vanilla sugar
food coloring in various colors

Preparation:

- Preheat the oven to 350°F/175°C.
- Place 24 muffin cups in a muffin pan.
- Whisk the margarine and sugar until white.
- Whisk in the eggs, one at a time.
- Add milk and flour and baking powder alternately.
- Add the vanilla extract.
- Fill the muffin cups about two-thirds full.
- Bake the cakes in the middle of the oven for about 20 minutes.
- Remove them from the oven, and cool the cupcakes in the pan for about 5 minutes. Move them onto a cooling rack, and let them cool completely.

THE FROSTING

- Stir the margarine until soft and smooth.
- Add vanilla extract. Sift in the powdered sugar and vanilla sugar, and add the milk a bit at a time. Add powdered sugar until the frosting is thick and spreadable.
- Add the food coloring, making pastel colors.

DECORATING

- Place the frosting in a decorating bag. Use tip no.6B.
- Decorate with fondant flowers, pastel colored sprinkles, and edible glitter.

Tip
Use vanilla sugar with real Bourbon vanilla.

VANILLA AND CARAMEL CUPCAKES

The combination of vanilla, walnuts, and caramel creates a taste to make any mouth water. Life is good when the soft caramel butter cream on these cupcakes is melting on your tongue.

{24 CUPCAKES}

You Need:

THE BATTER
4 eggs
1 ⅔ cups (338 g) sugar
1 cup (250 g) margarine,
    room temperature
1 cup (⅓ liter) milk
3 tsp baking powder
2 ½ cups (316 g) white
    all-purpose flour
1 ½ tsp vanilla extract
chopped walnuts
    (optional)

THE FROSTING
1 cup (250 g) margarine,
    room temperature
2 tsp vanilla extract
3 ½ tbsp milk
5 to 6 ¾ cups (608 to
    810 g) powdered sugar
caramel sauce, for
    flavoring

Preparation:

- Preheat the oven to 350°F/175°C.
- Place 24 muffin cups in a muffin pan.
- Stir margarine and sugar until white.
- Whisk in the eggs, one at a time.
- Add milk and flour and baking powder alternately.
- Chop the walnuts (choose your desired amount), and add them to the batter. Stir everything with a ladle.
- Add the vanilla extract.
- Fill the muffin cups about two-thirds full.
- Bake the cakes in the middle of the oven for about 20 minutes.
- Remove them from the oven, and leave in the pan to cool for about 5 minutes. Move the cupcakes onto a cooling rack, and let them cool completely.

THE FROSTING
- Stir the margarine until soft and smooth.
- Add the vanilla extract.
- Sift in the powdered sugar and vanilla sugar. Alternate by adding the milk. The frosting should be firm and spreadable.
- Flavor with caramel sauce.

DECORATING
- Place the frosting in a decorating bag. Use tip no. 1M.
- Color the fondant dark pink. Roll out the fondant thinly, maximum ¹⁄₁₆ inch thick. Use a spatula or a liner to cut the fondant into shreds. Place one over the other and tie so that the fondant forms a pink bow. Place the bow on top of the cupcake.

Tip
These are wonderful with some chopped walnuts on top as well.

AFTER EIGHT CUPCAKES

Cupcakes with a taste of After Eight are a sure winner. Treat yourself on a Friday night, or surprise guests with these tasty chocolate cupcakes. A well-deserved delight to kick-start the weekend.

{12 CUPCAKES}

You need:

THE BATTER
2 eggs
½ cup (100 g) margarine, room temperature
⅔ cup (126 g) sugar
1 ½ tsp baking powder
2 tsp coffee, cold
3.5 oz (100 g) dark chocolate
⅔ cup (80 g) white all-purpose flour
¼ cup (18 g) cocoa powder
12 pieces of After Eight or other after-dinner mint candy

THE FROSTING
2 oz (50 g) dark chocolate
10 pieces After Eight
3 to 6 tbsp (.8 to 1.7 fl oz) whipping cream

Preparation:

- Preheat the oven to 360°F/180°C.
- Place 12 muffin cups in a muffin pan.
- Stir eggs and sugar until white.
- Melt the chocolate and margarine separately. Use saucepans or melt them in the microwave.
- Blend the chocolate and margarine well, and let the blend cool.
- Stir the chocolate and margarine blend in with the egg and sugar mixture.
- Sift in flour, baking powder, and cocoa.
- Cut each of the After Eight squares into 4 to 6 pieces. Carefully turn them in the batter.
- Fill the cupcakes half full.
- Bake the cakes in the middle of the oven for about 20 minutes.
- Remove them from the oven, and cool them in the pan for about 5 minutes. Move them onto a cooling rack to cool completely.

THE FROSTING
- Pour all of the ingredients into a bowl and warm them in the microwave for 1 to 2 minutes.
- Stir well. This frosting should be more fluid-like.

DECORATING
- Use a spoon to dip the cupcake in the fluid chocolate topping.
- Decorate by sticking 1 After Eight in each cupcake. Remember that you need to do this before the chocolate glaze stiffens.

Tip
If you choose to use another kind of decoration, remember to decorate while the glaze is still soft and fluid. This way the decorations will stick better.

HELLO KITTY CUPCAKES

Hello Kitty is mostly popular among young girls and is usually a hit at birthdays. The orange flavor makes these cupcakes both fresh and sweet.

{12 CUPCAKES}

You need:

THE BATTER
2 eggs
1 cup + 2 tbsp (225 g) sugar
½ cup (115 g) margarine, room temperature
½ cup (60 g) white all-purpose flour
2 oranges
⅓ cup (60 g) semolina flour
½ tsp baking powder
⅔ cup (60 g) finely-ground almonds

THE ORANGE SYRUP
½ cup (100 g) sugar
1 cup (8 fl oz) water
the zest of 1 orange

THE FROSTING
1 stick (125 g) margarine, room temperature
8.8 oz, or a little over 1 cup (250 g) cream cheese
1 tsp vanilla extract
2 ½ to 3 cups (300 to 354 g) powdered sugar
1 tbsp freshly-squeezed lemon juice
1 tbsp lemon zest, grated

The Hello Kitty face is made out of fondant and placed on top of the frosting.

Preparation:

- Preheat the oven to 335°F/170°C.
- Place 12 muffin cups in a muffin pan.
- Peel the oranges and cut into small pieces.
- Place the orange pieces in a saucepan with water. The water should just barely cover the pieces. Bring to a boil and let it simmer for 15 to 20 minutes.
- Drain the water and stir until the fruit is completely dissolved.
- In a bowl, blend margarine, sugar, and oranges.
- Add the eggs, one at a time, and stir well after each one.
- Add sifted flour, semolina flour, and baking powder.
- Whisk everything for about 2 minutes (with a electric beater on medium speed), and turn in the finely ground almonds.
- Fill the muffin cups two-thirds full.
- Bake the cakes in the middle of the oven for 25 to 30 minutes.
- Cool in the muffin pan for about 5 minutes.

THE ORANGE SYRUP
- Grate the orange zest.
- Bring water and sugar to a boil, and add the grated zest. Stir for 5 to 7 minutes until all of the sugar has dissolved. Cool for about 10 minutes.
- Place the cupcakes on a cooling rack, and pour the syrup over them.

THE FROSTING
- Mix the margarine and cream cheese well.
- Add powdered sugar, lemon juice, lemon zest, and vanilla extract. Blend well.

DECORATING
- Place the frosting in a decorating bag. Use tip no. 1M.
- Squeeze out a thin layer of cream onto the cupcake.
- Roll out the white fondant to about 1⁄16 of an inch thick. Use a round cutter with a diameter of about 2 inches (5.5 cm). Roll a small yellow nose, black eyes, and white ears, and use a cutter to make a pink flower. Draw the three whiskers on each side with a black food marker.
- Place the finished fondant Hello Kitty figures on each cupcake.

EASTER CUPCAKES

Orange and chocolate are Easter classics in Norway. These orange and chocolate cupcakes are a wonderful combination of sweet and tart—just like chocolate orange wedges. Bring these cupcakes to any Easter dinner, and enjoy them as a family!

{8 CUPCAKES}

You need:

THE BATTER
2 eggs
1 cup (200 g) sugar
1 tsp vanilla extract
½ cup (115 g) margarine
½ tsp salt
2 ½ tsp baking powder
1 ½ cups (175 g) white
    all-purpose flour
½ cup (120 ml) orange
    juice
chocolate pieces

THE FROSTING
1 cup (100 g) powdered
    sugar
3.5 oz (100 g) dark choco-
    late, melted
½ stick (60 g) margarine
2 tbsp milk
1 tsp orange extract

Preparation:

- Preheat the oven to 350°F/175°C.
- Place 8 muffin cups in a muffin pan.
- Separate the egg whites and the yolks.
- Whisk the egg whites until fluffy, for 1 to 2 minutes.
- Stir vanilla extract, margarine, and sugar together.
- Add the yolks, one at a time.
- Add flour, salt, and baking powder, and alternate with orange juice.
- Fold in the egg whites.
- Add the chocolate pieces.
- Fill the muffin cups about two-thirds full.
- Bake the cakes in the middle of the oven for about 15 minutes.
- Remove them from the oven, and cool in the pan for about 5 minutes. Move the cupcakes onto a cooling rack, and let them cool completely.

THE FROSTING
- Melt chocolate over low heat. Continue stirring until it is all melted.
- Cool the blend. Add margarine and milk.
- Sift in powdered sugar, and add the orange extract. The frosting should have a firm texture.

DECORATING
- Spread the frosting on the cupcakes with tip no. 1B. To make grass use tip no. 233.
- Decorate with Easter decorations to look like Easter eggs, spring chickens, and so on.
- Roll out fondant with your fingers to make a spring chicken. Buy small chocolate eggs and spray them with edible color spray.

BAILEYS CUPCAKES

Baileys has a wonderful, silky flavor, and Baileys cupcakes are an exciting treat. Choose between five different flavors. These are excellent for the dessert table during Christmas or other holidays.

{20 CUPCAKES}

You need:

THE BATTER
2 eggs
1 stick (125 g) margarine, room temperature
1 ¼ cups (250 g) white sugar
½ cup (125 g) brown sugar
2 cups (264 g) white all-purpose flour
1 ½ cups (125 g) cocoa powder
2 tsp vanilla extract
¼ tsp salt
1 ½ tsp baking powder
½ cup (130 g) sour cream
1 ½ cups (13 fl oz) Baileys (original)

THE FROSTING
3.5 oz (100 g) cream cheese
1 cup (250 g) margarine, room temperature
5 to 6 cups (608 to 700 g) powdered sugar
8 to 10 tbsp Baileys (choose between five different flavors)

Preparation:

- Preheat the oven to 350°F/175°C.
- Place 20 muffin cups in two muffin pans.
- Stir the margarine and sugar until light and airy.
- Add the eggs, one at a time. Whisk well between each one.
- Add the vanilla extract.
- In a separate bowl, sift flour, cocoa powder, baking powder, and salt.
- Add Baileys and sour cream to the margarine blend, and alternate with milk.
- Whisk everything with an electric beater on medium speed.
- Fill the muffin cups two-thirds full.
- Bake the cakes in the middle of the oven for about 20 minutes.
- Remove them from the oven, and cool them in the pan for about 5 minutes. Let the cupcakes cool completely on a cooling rack.

THE FROSTING
- Whisk margarine, cream cheese, and powdered sugar.
- Fold in the Baileys. The frosting should have a firm, spreadable texture.

DECORATING
- Use tip no. 2D.
- Sprinkle gold marbles and other décor on the cupcakes.

Tip
If you prefer not to use alcohol, you can replace the Baileys in the frosting with 8 to 10 tbsp chocolate sauce.

BANANA AND CHOCOLATE CUPCAKES

Mothers deserve something extra special. Why not surprise your mom with a cupcake gift this Mother's Day? Banana and chocolate is a perfect flavor combination. These are moist and full of love!

{24 CUPCAKES}

You need:

THE BATTER

3 eggs
1 cup (210 g) white sugar
⅓ cup (92 g) brown sugar
¾ cup (175 ml) vegetable oil
2 ½ tsp vanilla extract
1 tbsp cinnamon
1 tsp salt
1 tsp baking soda
½ tsp baking powder
4 large and ripe bananas
3 cups (370 g) white
   all-purpose flour
5 oz, or a little over ¾ cup
   (142 g) chocolate chips

THE FROSTING

1 cup (250 g) margarine,
   room temperature
3 oz (80 g) cream cheese
1 cup (80 g) cocoa powder
5-7 tbsp chocolate sauce
   (optional)
3 ½ tbsp whole milk
5 to 6 ¾ cups (507 to 676 g)
   powdered sugar, sifted

Preparation:

- Preheat the oven to 360°F/180°C.
- Place 24 muffin cups in 2 muffin pans.
- Whisk the eggs and sugar until fluffy.
- Add vanilla extract, cinnamon, salt, baking soda, and baking powder.
- Sift in the flour, and add the oil alternately. Whisk into a fluffy batter.
- Add mashed bananas.
- Add the chocolate chips.
- Fill the muffin cups two-thirds full.
- Bake the cakes in the middle of the oven for 20 to 25 minutes.
- Remove them from the oven, and cool them in the pan for about 5 minutes. Place the cupcakes on a cooling rack, and let them cool completely.

THE FROSTING

- Stir margarine, cream cheese, and cocoa powder together. Add the chocolate sauce if desired.
- Add the powdered sugar and milk alternately, a little at a time.
- Whisk with an electric beater on medium speed until everything is blended well. Increase the speed to high for the last 2 minutes to make the frosting as fluffy as possible. Add additional powdered sugar if desired.

DECORATING

- Use a decorating bag and tip no. 8B.
- Roll out fondant and use a cutter to make the tag. Write "Mother" or "Mom" with a jelly pen. Feel free to add some pearls around the edge of the fondant tag.
- Top it off by sprinkling the same pearls around the cupcake.

GRANDMA'S BUTTERFLY CUPCAKES

I love Grandma's butterfly cupcakes! They are stylish and decorative, and they work for any occasion. Picture a lovely dessert table in the yard on a quiet summer night, overflowing with butterfly cupcakes dressed in their finest!

{12 CUPCAKES}

You need:

THE BATTER
2 eggs
1 stick (125 g) margarine
2 ⅓ cups (300 g) white
 all-purpose flour, sifted
⅔ cup (125 g) sugar
2 tsp baking powder
⅓ cup (5 tbsp) milk
1 tsp vanilla extract

THE CREAM
whipped cream

Preparation:

- Preheat the oven to 390°F/200°C.
- Place 12 muffin cups in a muffin pan.
- Stir the margarine and sugar until white.
- Whisk the eggs in a separate bowl, and add them to the batter.
- Add flour and baking powder.
- Stir in the milk and the vanilla extract.
- Fill the muffin cups about two-thirds full.
- Bake the cakes in the middle of the oven for 10 to 15 minutes.
- Remove them from the oven, and cool them in the pan for 5 minutes. Place the cupcakes on a cooling rack, and let them cool completely.
- Cut the top off of every cupcake.

DECORATING
- It is very important that the cupcakes have risen properly in the oven and that they have a significant top.
- Cut the top off the cupcakes and slice in two.
- Cover the bottom part of the cupcake with whipped cream.
- Place the two parts in the cream like butterfly wings.
- Add colorful butterflies made out of fondant.
- To make butterflies roll out the fondant to about ¹⁄₁₆ inch thick. Use a cutter in a butterfly shape. Use a brush and edible glitter dust to decorate the butterflies in the colors you prefer. Place silver marbles at the middle of the butterflies to shape the body. Lastly, place the butterflies in a pan so that they "dry" and the wings obtain a V-shape.

ESPRESSO CUPCAKES

How about a delicious cupcake on your coffee break? Espresso cupcakes are wonderful and a great alternative to the regular cup of coffee. Sit down, relax, and enjoy this lovely blend of cream cheese and coffee. You deserve a little break.

{12 CUPCAKES}

You need:

THE BATTER

1 egg
¾ cup (150 g) sugar
10 tbsp vegetable oil
1 tsp cinnamon
1 ½ tbsp espresso powder
1 ½ cups (180 g) white all-purpose flour
2 tsp baking powder
⅔ cup (171 g) plain yogurt
2 oz, or around ⅓ cup (50 g) chocolate chips

THE FROSTING

1 stick (125 g) margarine, room temperature
1 ½ oz (40 g) cream cheese
½ cup (40 g) cocoa powder
1 ¾ tbsp milk
2 ½ to 3 ⅓ cups (300 to 405 g) powdered sugar
2 to 3 tbsp chocolate sauce
1 to 1 ½ tbsp espresso powder

Preparation:

- Preheat the oven to 360°F/180°C.
- Place 12 muffin cups in a muffin pan.
- Blend sugar, baking powder, espresso powder, and cinnamon in a bowl. Remember to sift everything.
- In a separate bowl, whisk eggs, oil, and yogurt.
- Add the egg blend to the dry mixture, a little at the time.
- Stir in the chocolate chips.
- Fill the muffin cups two-thirds full.
- Bake the cakes in the middle of the oven for 20 to 25 minutes.
- Remove them from the oven, and cool them in the pan for about 5 minutes. Place the cupcakes on a cooling rack, and let them cool completely.

THE FROSTING

- Mix all of the ingredients and whisk them with an electric beater for about 2 minutes on medium speed. Increase the speed and whisk for an additional 2 minutes.

DECORATING

- Place the frosting in a decorating bag. Use tip no. 1M.
- Squeeze out a thick layer of frosting, start on the outer edge, and work your way inwards in circular movements.
- Decorate with sifted cocoa powder.

Tip
You may also decorate with espresso beans.

COSMOPOLITAN CUPCAKES

These cosmopolitan cupcakes are just as delicious as they look. If you are up for a challenge, make these. Decorate them in pearls and accessories and make them the talk of the party.

{22 CUPCAKES}

You need:

THE BATTER
2 eggs
⅔ cup (150 g) margarine, room temperature
1 ⅔ cups (338 g) sugar
½ tsp salt
3 tsp baking powder
3 cups (396 g) white all-purpose flour, sifted
4 tbsp sour milk
1 ¼ cups (10.5 fl oz) cosmopolitan (the drink)*
grated zest of 1 lime

THE FROSTING
1 cup (250 g) margarine, room temperature
5 to 6 cups (507 to 676 g) powdered sugar, sifted
a pinch of salt
1 tsp lime zest
3 to 6 tbsp cosmopolitan drink mix (with alcohol)
pink food coloring
1 tbsp meringue powder (optional)

*COSMOPOLITAN (THE DRINK)
1.5 fl oz (45 ml) vodka
2.5 fl oz (80 ml) Cointreau
1 fl oz (30 ml) freshly-squeezed lime juice
1 cup (230 ml) cranberry juice

Preparation:

- Preheat the oven to 350°F/175°C.
- Place 22 muffin cups in two muffin pans.
- Make cosmopolitan (the drink).
- Stir margarine and sugar until white.
- Add the eggs, one at a time, whisking well after each one.
- Add lime zest, and stir well.
- In a separate bowl sift all-purpose flour, baking powder, and salt.
- Add the cosmopolitan and the flour blend to the margarine mix, alternating. Add the sour milk.
- Stir well on low speed.
- Fill the muffin cups two-thirds full.
- Bake the cakes in the middle of the oven for about 20 minutes.
- Remove them from the oven, and cool them in the pan for 5 minutes.
- Before the cupcakes have cooled completely, brush them with the cosmopolitan liquid.

THE FROSTING
- Whisk together margarine, sifted powdered sugar, salt, and lime zest.
- Add cosmopolitan drink mix, 1 tsp at a time, until the frosting has a firm texture.
- Add the pink fool coloring. Make some of the cupcakes a brighter pink than the others. Color nuances look great on a plate.

DECORATING
- Use a decorating bag and tip no. 8B.
- Squeeze out a thick layer of frosting. Start at the outer edge and work your way inwards in circular movements. The frosting should be tall.
- Use pink mini-pearls and edible glitter for an extra shiny effect.

Tip
If you want the cupcakes to be alcohol-free, use cranberry juice instead of the drink mix.

CRÈME DE MENTHE CUPCAKES

Give you father a small treat with these delicious cupcakes on Father's Day. The mint and chocolate flavor never fails when it is time to celebrate Dad!

{12 CUPCAKES}

You need:

THE BATTER
4 eggs
1 cup (225 g) margarine
1 cup (200 g) sugar
1 ½ tsp baking powder
1 ⅓ cups (180 g) white all-purpose flour, sifted
4 tbsp cocoa powder
1 tsp mint extract
3.5 oz, or a little over ½ cup (100 g) mint chocolates

THE FROSTING
⅔ cup (150 g) margarine, room temperature
2 to 4 tbsp Crème de menthe
2 ½ to 3 ⅓ cups (253 to 338g) powdered sugar, sifted food coloring

Preparation:

- Preheat the oven to 350°F/175°C.
- Place 12 muffin cups in two muffin pans.
- Stir sugar and margarine until white. Add the eggs, one at a time, and stir well.
- In a separate bowl, blend flour, baking powder, and cocoa powder.
- Add the dry ingredients to the batter, a little at a time.
- Add the mint chocolates and mint extract. Whisk well.
- Fill the muffin cups two-thirds full.
- Bake the cakes in the oven for about 20 minutes.
- Remove them from the oven, and cool them in a muffin pan for about 5 minutes. Place the cupcakes on a cooling rack, and cool completely.

THE FROSTING
- Stir powdered sugar and margarine until white.
- Add green food coloring until it is pastel in color.
- Add Crème de menthe.

DECORATING
- Use a decorating bag to distribute the frosting. Use tip no. 4B.
- Sprinkle 3.5 oz (100 g) chocolate bits on top.
- Roll out white fondant to about ¹⁄₁₆ inch thick. Use a large flower-shaped cutter to cut out the flower motif. Spray the fondant with white pearl spray for a glittering effect.
- Write "Dad" on the fondant tag with a jelly pen. Let the writing dry.
- Place the fondant tag vertically across the top of the cupcake.

APPLE CUPCAKES

Apple cake is a favorite of many. Next time try it in a cupcake variety. The cinnamon sprinkle gives a sweet, spiced flavor that complements the apples perfectly.

{12 CUPCAKES}

You need:

THE BATTER

1 egg
⅓ cup (60 g) sugar
2 cups (250 g) white all-purpose flour
½ tsp salt
2 tsp baking powder
2 to 3 tbsp honey
¾ cup + 1 ½ tbsp (⅕ liter) whole milk
1 ⅓ cups (150 g) apple slices
brown sugar and cinnamon as a topping

FROSTING

whipped cream

Preparation:

- Preheat the oven to 360°F/180°C.
- Place 12 muffin cups in a muffin pan.
- Slice the apples.
- Add sugar and egg to a bowl, and stir well. Add honey and the apple slices. Continue stirring.
- In a separate bow, sift flour, baking powder, and salt.
- Pour the apple blend and the milk alternately into the dry ingredients. Carefully stir.
- Fill the muffin cups two-thirds full.
- Sprinkle brown sugar and cinnamon on top.
- Bake in the oven for 20 to 25 minutes.
- Remove them from the oven, and cool them in the pan for about 5 minutes. Cool the cupcakes completely on a cooling rack.

Decorating
- Only one-fourth of the cupcake should be covered in whipping cream, so make a small peak that only covers some of the cake.
- Decorate with a flower.

NEW YEAR'S EVE CUPCAKES

New Year's Eve is a celebration and the perfect occasion to serve these gorgeous party cupcakes. These, with Ferrero Rochet chocolate, will definitely satisfy the tastes of both adults and children. They taste heavenly! Decorate the cupcakes to match the table! Happy New Year!

{12 CUPCAKES}

You need:

THE BATTER

2 eggs
6 tbsp white sugar
10 tbsp brown sugar
1 cup (125 g) white all-
    purpose flour, sifted
1 tsp baking powder
¼ cup milk
1 tbsp vanilla extract
1 tbsp hazelnut extract
½ cup (115 g) margarine,
    room temperature
½ cup (3.5 fl oz) water,
    boiling
¼ tsp salt
6 tbsp cocoa powder
Nutella (hazelnut spread)

THE FROSTING

2 tbsp light syrup
1 tbsp hazelnut extract
7 tbsp (1.7 fl oz) whipping
    cream
6 oz, or 1 ⅓ cups grated
    (175 g) baking chocolate
1 ⅓ cups (150 g) crushed
    hazelnuts

Preparation:

- Preheat the oven to 350°F/175°C.
- Place 12 muffin cups in a muffin pan.
- Stir the margarine and sugar until soft and fluffy.
- Add the eggs, one at a time, and whisk well between each one.
- Bring water to a boil, and stir in sifted coca powder. Stir well.
- Stir milk, hazelnut extract, and vanilla extract into the cocoa blend. Carefully mix with a hand beater.
- In a separate bowl, blend flour, baking powder, and salt.
- Alternately add the cocoa blend and the flour blend to the batter. Whisk everything on medium speed for about 3 minutes until the batter has a smooth and even texture.
- Fill the muffin cups about two-thirds full.
- Bake the cakes in the middle of the oven for about 20 minutes.
- Remove them from the oven and cool them in the pan for about 5 minutes. Place the cupcakes on a cooling rack to cool completely.
- Make a hole in the middle of the cupcake. Use an olive pitter, but make sure that you do not make a hole all the way through.
- Use a decorating bag to fill the hole with Nutella.

THE FROSTING

- Blend the syrup and melted chocolate. Stir well.
- Warm the whipping cream in a saucepan on medium heat for about 2 minutes.
- Stir the hazelnut extract in with the chocolate blend, and add the cream. Stir well. Let the blend rest for a couple of minutes.
- Add the crushed hazelnuts.

DECORATING

- Wait until the cupcakes are completely cool before you start decorating.
- Dip the cupcakes in the chocolate frosting.
- Decorate with shooting stars, gold glitter sprinkles, and crushed hazelnuts. Decorate any way to match the party table.

BLUEBERRY CUPCAKES

Blueberries contain healthy antioxidants and they also taste amazingly fresh. Blueberries and cupcakes are a natural combination and are just as fitting in the lunchbox as in the picnic basket, or for afternoon coffee. Healthy and tasty.

{24 CUPCAKES}

You need:

THE BATTER
2 eggs
3 cups (370 g) powdered sugar
⅓ cup (70 g) margarine, room temperature
3 cups (360 g) white all-purpose flour, sifted
1 tsp salt
½ tsp baking soda
1 ½ tsp baking powder
2 tsp vanilla extract
1 ½ cups (6.4 fl oz) whipping cream
½ lb (250 g) fresh blueberries

THE FROSTING
1 stick (125 g) margarine, room temperature
1 tsp vanilla extract
¼ cup milk
2 ½ to 3 ⅓ cups (300 to 405 g) powdered sugar
lemon juice for flavor
food coloring

Preparation:

- Preheat the oven to 350°F/175°C.
- Place 24 muffin cups in 2 muffin pans.
- Whisk margarine, powdered sugar, and vanilla extract, while also adding one egg at a time.
- In a separate bowl blend flour, salt, baking soda, and baking powder.
- Stir the dry ingredients into the batter. Add the whipping cream, and whisk well with a mixer.
- Carefully turn in the blueberries.
- Fill the cupcakes about two-thirds full.
- Bake the cakes in the middle of the oven for about 15 minutes.
- Remove them from the oven, and cool them in the pan for 5 minutes. Continue to cool the cupcakes on a cooling rack.

THE FROSTING
- Stir the margarine until soft and smooth.
- Add the vanilla extract. Sift in powdered sugar and alternate by adding the milk. Add enough powdered sugar so that the frosting is firm and spreadable.
- Flavor with lemon juice.
- Add food coloring in pastel colors.

DECORATING
- Use a decorating bag and tip no. 1C.
- Sprinkle fresh blueberries on top or arrange just three blueberries on top.

CARROT CUPCAKES

On Halloween we dress up and scare our neighbors into giving us candy. At least the children do. Cupcakes are a given on Halloween, with loads of decorating options—with the traditional black and orange color themes as the base. They may look quite unfriendly but they taste great.

{24 CUPCAKES}

You need:

THE BATTER

⅓ cup (84 g) white sugar
⅓ cup (92 g) brown sugar
1 ¾ sticks (200 g) margarine
2 eggs
½ tsp salt
2 tsp cinnamon
2 tsp baking powder
1 cup (⅕ liter) milk
2 ¾ cups (342 g) white all-purpose flour, sifted
1 cup (123 g) walnuts (optional)
2 carrots, grated

THE FROSTING

12 oz or 1 ½ cups (350 g) cream cheese
1 ¾ sticks (200 g) margarine
4 cups (500 g) powdered sugar
3 tbsp vanilla sugar

Preparation:

- Preheat the oven to 390°F/200°C.
- Place 24 muffin cups in two muffin pans.
- Stir margarine and sugar until fluffy.
- In a separate bowl, blend flour, cinnamon, salt, and baking powder. Add the eggs, one at a time, whisking well between each one.
- Pour the milk into the margarine and sugar mixture, alternating the milk and the egg blend.
- Grate carrots and chop the walnuts finely. Add them to the batter and carefully stir.
- Fill the muffin cups about two-thirds full.
- Bake the cupcakes in the middle of the oven for 15 to 20 minutes.
- Remove them from the oven, and cool in the pan for about 5 minutes. Let them cool completely on a cooling rack.

THE FROSTING

- Whisk margarine, cream cheese, powdered sugar, and vanilla sugar for 3 to 4 minutes on medium speed.

DECORATING

- Place the frosting in a decorating bag. Use tips nos. 1C and 8B.
- Make orange, black, and green cupcakes by spraying them with color spray. Buy Halloween decorations from any candy or grocery store.
- To make pumpkins: Roll out an orange fondant ball. Use a flower-shaped cutter to make the green stem. Gently press the pumpkin so that it takes on an oval shape. Use a toothpick to make the stripes.
- To make a ghost: Roll out white fondant, about 1/16 inch thick. Use a round cutter with about a 5- to 7-inch (14- to 16-cm) diameter. You may also use a cup. Place the fondant over the cupcakes with frosting underneath. Draw the mouth and eyes on the ghost.

WHITE CHOCOLATE CUPCAKES

Cupcakes can be adorable and cute and perfect for baby showers. Here you may have fun decorating with lovely baby decorations and muffin cups. Both old and young will love these.

{12 CUPCAKES}

You need:

THE BATTER

2 eggs, separate the yolk from the egg white
1 cup (200 g) light brown sugar
1 ½ cups (200 g) white all-purpose flour
3 tsp baking powder
1 cup (225 g) margarine, room temperature
3.5 oz (100 g) dark chocolate, melted
1 tsp vanilla extract
½ cup milk

THE FROSTING

1 stick (125 g) margarine, room temperature
3 tbsp milk
1 cup (200 g) white chocolate, melted
1 tbsp vanilla extract
3 cups (300 g) powdered sugar, sifted

Preparation:

- Preheat the oven to 350°F/175°C.
- Place 12 muffin cups in a muffin pan.
- Melt the chocolate in the microwave or in a water bath.
- Stir the margarine and sugar until soft using a mixer.
- Add the yolks, one at a time (the egg whites will be added later).
- Add vanilla extract and melted chocolate. Continue whisking on medium speed.
- Sift flour and baking powder into a bowl.
- Add the dry mixture and the milk alternately to the margarine and chocolate blend.
- Whip the egg whites until stiff, and carefully fold them in the batter.
- Fill the muffin cups two-thirds full.
- Bake the cakes in the middle of the oven for about 20 minutes.
- Remove them from the oven, and cool them in the pan for about 5 minutes. Allow them to cool completely on a cooling rack.

THE FROSTING

- Blend margarine, white chocolate, vanilla extract, and milk. Sift in the powdered sugar. Whisk the frosting until creamy and spreadable.

DECORATING

- Make half of the frosting light blue with food color from Wilton. Keep the other half white.
- Use a decorating bag and tip no. 1C.
- Start on the outer edge and work your way inwards.
- Make baby figures with silicone shapes. Press the fondant into the shapes to make bottles, strollers, teddy bears, and so on.
- With a brush and edible glitter dust, decorate the figures with colors of your choice.
- Make flowers with cutters and colored fondant.
- The remaining cupcakes should be decorated with pearls and glitter dust.

COFFEE AND WALNUT CUPCAKES

Cupcakes belong in every festive occasion. What about these coffee and walnut cupcakes for a Superbowl- or Oscar-viewing party?

{12 CUPCAKES}

You need:

THE BATTER

4 eggs
1 cup (200 g) sugar
1 cup (225 g) margarine,
    room temperature
1 ½ cups (200 g) white
    all-purpose flour, sifted
3 tsp baking powder
1 tsp instant coffee
1 cup (100 g) walnuts,
    chopped
2 carrots, grated
2 tbsp yellow raisins

THE FROSTING

4 oz or ½ cup (120 g)
    cream cheese, room
    temperature
4 cups (400 g) powdered
    sugar, sifted
2 tsp coffee liqueur
2 to 3 tbsp freshly-brewed
    coffee, cooled

6 tbsp walnuts, chopped

Preparation:

- Preheat the oven to 350°F/175°C.
- Place 12 muffin cups in muffin pans.
- Whisk margarine and sugar until white and creamy.
- Add the eggs, one at a time. Whisk for 2 to 3 minutes.
- Sift in flour, baking powder, and instant coffee.
- Turn in the grated carrots, chopped walnuts, and yellow raisins.
- Fill the muffin cups two-thirds full.
- Bake the cakes in the middle of the oven for about 20 minutes.
- Remove them from the oven, and cool in the pan for 5 minutes. Allow them to cool completely on a cooling rack.

THE FROSTING

- Whisk together cream cheese, powdered sugar, and coffee.
- Fold in the liqueur.

DECORATING

- Place the frosting in a decorating bag. Use tip no. 1A.
- Start on the outer edge and work your way inwards in a circle.
- Roll the edge of the cupcake in chopped walnuts.

Tip
If you want a rather different flavor you can replace the cream cheese with mascarpone cheese.

CARAMEL CUPCAKES WITH PECANS

Gather family and close friends for an enjoyable fall party and enjoy the world's most lovely cupcakes. Wonderful with delicious, flowing caramel sauce and pecans.

{16 CUPCAKES}

You need:

THE BATTER

4 eggs
⅔ cup (126 g) white sugar
⅔ cup (140 g) brown sugar
1 ¾ sticks (200 g) margarine, room temperature
1 ½ tsp baking powder
1 tsp cinnamon
½ tsp cardamom
1 ⅔ cups (211 g) white all-purpose flour, sifted
mocha extract
½ cup (96 g) almond meal
1 ¼ cups (5 fl oz) whipping cream
3 cups (300 g) pecans
1 ripe banana (optional)

THE CARAMEL SAUCE

½ stick (60 g) margarine, room temperature
½ cup (100 g) light brown sugar
4 tbsp light syrup
⅔ cup (2.5 fl oz) whipping cream

Preparation:

- Preheat the oven to 360°F/180°C.
- Brown the nuts in the oven for about 15 minutes.
- Cool on a cooling rack.
- Place 16 muffin cups in a muffin pan.
- Whisk margarine and sugar until light and soft.
- Add cinnamon and cardamom.
- Flavor the batter with mocha extract—you only need a few drops. Continue whisking till everything is blended well.
- When the pecans are cool, save about half of them for decorating.
- The remaining half should be chopped into small pieces.
- Leave the chopped nuts for now.
- Sift all-purpose flour, baking powder, and almond meal into a bowl.
- Add the flour blend to the batter. Whisk for a couple of minutes.
- Add the whipping cream, and whisk some more.
- Add the mashed banana.
- Fold in the chopped pecans.
- Fill the muffin cups two-thirds full.
- Bake the cakes in the middle of the oven for 15 minutes.
- Remove them from the oven, and cool them in the muffin pan for 5 minutes. Cool completely on a cooling rack.

THE CARAMEL SAUCE

- Place margarine, syrup, and brown sugar in a saucepan.
- Warm while constantly stirring. If the sauce starts to bubble, it is perfect. Continue to stir for 2 minutes more.
- Add the cream, and stir until the mass thickens.
- Let the sauce cool for about 5 minutes.

DECORATING

- In this recipe the sauce is very fluid. You can, optionally, use extra-tall muffin cups to avoid sauce spilling over the sides.
- Place pecan nuts—whole or chopped—on the cupcakes.
- Pour the caramel sauce over the nuts.

BERRY CUPCAKES (LACTOSE FREE)

Try this fresh and tasty cupcake recipe without milk. Also recommended for those who can tolerate milk products.

{12 CUPCAKES}

You need:

THE BATTER

2 eggs
2 ⅔ cups (375 g) berries,
  fresh or frozen (strawberries, blackberries, cranberries, or blueberries)
½ cup (115 g) brown sugar
3 tbsp cocoa powder
3 tbsp vegetable oil
1 tbsp baking powder
2 cups (225 g) white all-purpose flour, sifted

DECORATING

fresh berries

Preparation:

- Preheat the oven to 350°F/175°C.
- Place 12 muffin cups in a muffin pan.
- Stir the berries together.
- Whisk eggs and oil.
- Sift in half of the flour and the baking powder.
- Add the sugar and cocoa powder. Stir well.
- Add half of the berry blend. Stir well.
- Sift in the remainder of the flour and the rest of the berries.
- Fill the muffin cups about two-thirds full.
- Bake them in the oven for about 20 minutes.
- Remove them for the oven, and cool them in the pan for 5 minutes. Allow them to cool completely on a cooling rack.

DECORATING

- As a topping you may use 1 tbsp homemade jam or some fresh berries.

A warm thank you to

Mommy Bronwyn and Daddy Aksel for all their support of my ideas and inventions over the years, as well as the good advice, help, positive enthusiasm, and able guidance along the way. Thank you to my brother, Anders, and my sister, Mari, who are always positive promoters and provide constant inspiration to the furthering of Hancock Cupcakes. Thank you to Grandpa, Grandma, and Auntie, who have always encouraged me to never give up and to have faith in myself. A thank you also to my dear Erik Andre, who is always patient and loving and believes that my dreams can come true. Without the support of those closest to me, Hancock Cupcakes would have never been the success it is today.

A special thanks to

Editor Bente Dahl Svendsen, who has shown me trust and inspired me to write this book. Thank you for all the advice, positive energy, and motivation along the way. Thank you to photographer Marte Garmann for lovely pictures and wonderful styling. A thank you to Hege Cecilie Nordli for the help with decorating these beautiful cupcakes, and for great guidance, tips, and advice along the way. Thank you to Astrid and Ola Brathseth for all your help and motivation.

Thank you to every contributor to this book!